SURVIVING
COVID-19

HOW FAITH, FOCUS, FITNESS, AND HYDROXYCHLOROQUINE SAVED ME

Dan Venezia
WITH FREDERICK RICHARDSON

Post Hill
PRESS

A POST HILL PRESS BOOK
ISBN: 978-1-64293-748-0
ISBN (eBook): 978-1-64293-749-7

Surviving COVID-19:
How Faith, Focus, Fitness, and Hydroxychloroquine Saved Me
© 2020 by Dan Venezia
All Rights Reserved

Cover art by Cody Corcoran
Cover photo and author photo by Jose Fernandez, JFZ Photography

This is a work of nonfiction. All people, locations, events, and situations are portrayed to the best of the author's memory.

Post Hill Press
New York • Nashville
posthillpress.com

Published in the United States of America

This book is dedicated to my wife, Heather.
Thank you for always being in my corner
—you are beautiful inside and out.

And to my sons, Ryan and Skyler
—I am so proud of the young men you have become.
I love you all so much.

CONTENTS

Chapter One   Palm Sunday, 2020 1

Chapter Two   Brooklyn Beginnings 9

Chapter Three   Nothing Good Comes Easy 27

Chapter Four   Every Boy's Dream 36

Chapter Five   Head-On 52

Chapter Six   One Dream Ends................................. 63

Chapter Seven   Another Dream Begins 77

Chapter Eight   Forgiveness 88

Chapter Nine   A Father's Guidance........................... 112

Chapter Ten   Becoming a Father............................. 126

Chapter Eleven   Be Fair. Play Hard.............................. 143

Chapter Twelve   Shaping Lives...................................... 161

Chapter Thirteen   Newfound Faith 173

Chapter Fourteen   COVID-19—Faith, Focus, Fitness, and Hydroxychloroquine................... 188

Chapter Fifteen   Easter Sunday—Resurrection............. 202

Acknowledgments.. 209

About the Author 215

CHAPTER ONE

PALM SUNDAY, 2020

"During challenging times, we should never feel sorry for ourselves. Jesus never felt sorry for himself."

Monsignor Geno Sylva, my dear friend and parish priest of our home church, said these words in his Palm Sunday homily. On a typical Palm Sunday, my wife, Heather, my two boys, Ryan and Skyler, and I would have been sitting in our customary pew in the Cathedral of St. John the Baptist in Paterson, New Jersey. We would be at the beginning of Holy Week—that most important season in the church year when we enter Jerusalem with Jesus on Palm Sunday, go into the upper room with his disciples for the institution of the Lord's Supper on Holy Thursday, observe his death on the cross on Good Friday, try to imagine life without the resurrection on Holy Saturday, and then glory in the miracle of his empty tomb on Easter Sunday.

But this was no typical Palm Sunday. The church was empty; Msgr. Geno's homily beamed to us by satellite and was captured in our separate homes, our separate rooms, through Wi-Fi. Like everyone else, I was listening to his homily at home. But unlike most, I wasn't able to listen with my family. Rather than sitting snuggled in a pew with the love of my life beside

1

me, I was quarantined, walled off from my family because of my confirmed diagnosis of COVID-19. Those words from our priest were all that my mind, wracked for ten days by a constantly pounding headache, was able to absorb. But thank God it did. I would need those words to sustain me and give me hope in the coming days.

After virtual church, I lay in bed, tortured for the fourteenth day by aches and pains, suffering for the eleventh straight day with a fever of 103 degrees. As the day wore on, my breathing came with greater and greater difficulty. I had one of those gadgets on my index finger to check for oxygen levels, which I began to monitor more and more closely. My childhood asthma seemed to have returned with a vengeance. I finally decided that I needed a professional opinion as to whether or not it was time for me to seek medical attention. I called Dr. Charles Thorne, a good friend and one of New York City's top plastic surgeons, who was now, like many other specialists, on the front lines with the nurses and other practitioners fighting this deadly pandemic. He told me to get to the emergency room. Immediately.

I drove myself.

When I was finally seen, the emergency room doctor played his infield halfway in with a runner on third base. At least, from my worldview of life as a baseball game, that's how I saw it. For those unfamiliar, this is what an unsure coach does who can't decide—do I have my team play in and try to get the runner out at the plate; or do I play them back, give up the run, but get the out? By playing his infield only halfway in, he may end up costing his team the run and still not get the out.

"Do you want us to check you into the hospital, or do you want to be released and go home?"

Why was I having to make that decision? Wasn't that his job?

In that moment of fevered lunacy and mind-numbing pain, I said I needed some time. He seemed a bit confused by my response.

"How much time do you need?" he awkwardly asked.

"Five minutes," I replied.

The words of my wise father-in-law, now gone to be with the Lord, came to me. "Trust your gut, it's usually right."

My gut told me that I wanted to be at home, in my bed, with my family near me. Who in their right mind would choose being in a hospital filled with dying COVID-19 patients rather than being back at home? But I wasn't in my right mind. Then, I heard more words of wisdom from my father-in-law. "If someone can convince you that you're wrong, you should change your mind. In fact, you must change your mind."

I called Dr. Thorne again. This was the lifeline I needed, "Call a Friend," like I was on the old game show, *Who Wants to Be a Millionaire?* He answered my call immediately.

"They gave me a choice to stay the night or go home. Should I stay or should I go?" I asked.

He gave a direct, reassuring answer, the answer a good coach would give.

Infield in! We are not giving up the run.

"You should stay put in the hospital." Dr. Thorne was decisive. He gave sound, practical medical advice as to why I was better off in the hospital. They could do more for me there than I could do for myself at home.

"It's only going to be one night," I said to myself.

And then I prayed a simple prayer.

"Please God, let them give me the hydroxychloroquine. Maybe I will sleep better tonight."

Almost immediately a different doctor, young and female, entered the small room at the corner of the ER. "We are going to give you hydroxychloroquine."

I smiled for the first time in two weeks.

Wow! That prayer got answered fast!

They put me in a wheelchair, took me down a short corridor, then made a left to the elevator banks. We headed up to the second floor. After getting off the elevator, we took another left turn, and I was wheeled down a long corridor until we took a right-hand turn into the COVID-19 wing.

"Am I able to get a private room?" I asked.

Like far too many others, I was unemployed at the moment because of the pandemic. Sure, a private room would cost more, but I wasn't thinking about the money.

What's one more bill piled on top of the rest that have been coming in?

"Sorry, sir, we only have one spot available—it's in room 2343."

As the tech rolled me down the hall, I heard a loud cough. The closer we got to the room, the louder and more agonizing my future roommate's cough sounded.

There was no introduction—we were both too sick to introduce ourselves. And I was absolutely wrong about getting a better night's sleep. The dry cough coming from my neighbor was deafening. The beeps coming from the monitor, along with the latest news from the TV coming through the speaker on the little remote control lost somewhere on my bed, made my pounding headache worse. Fitful moments of delirious uncon-sciousness was about the best I could do.

Then there was the sound of my own wheezy breathing, which was getting shallower by the minute. Beginning at around 2 a.m., I noticed that the clock didn't seem to be budging. Maybe it was broken? Even if I could have found the remote and pushed the button to call the nurse, I didn't think I should ask her. Determining the time of day (or night, whichever it was) was not a priority for someone taking care of people with my condition.

I finally mustered up enough strength to find that darn remote control, which was stuck in the crease of the bed around my L-4 or L-5 vertebrae area, a place that throbbed with pain.

I heard the muffled sound of the news, talking about people who were infected. I realized that they were, in fact, talking about me. My mind drifted as I laid there in the hospital bed, COVID-19 coursing through my body.

For a time, I forgot Msgr. Geno's words from earlier that day. With time standing still, the temptation came to go into a dark place—a place of anxiety, frustration, doubt. Would I give in and even question God?

I am usually the optimist, picking others up. But I couldn't pick anyone or anything up at the moment. Even the tape holding my IV in place hurt.

That was no match, though, for the pain caused by the intravenous cannula. It felt like an oversized pencil, twisting and turning, trying to fit into a vein that was too small. I tried to focus on the lesser pain, the tape that held the dagger down.

Maybe if I pulled the tape off, it would provide some relief?

I tried, but the headache came back, distracting me from my obsession with the IV.

I needed something for the headache.

I needed to know if the darn clock was broken.

I needed ice water.

A little man inside my head kept swinging away with that sledgehammer, over and over again.

I tried to keep my eyes closed as I watched the news, or at least heard it coming from the little remote control in my bed. I was fixated on that darn clock, right next to the television. Was it still only 2 a.m.? Was I dreaming? Having a nightmare?

I opened my eyes, and the local news showed overcrowded morgues and bodies in nursing homes. An image of families unable to have viewings and proper funerals for their loved ones hovered over my head. They spoke about how the most vulnerable were the elderly, along with those with underlying conditions.

I'm forty-eight; certainly not among the elderly, but I do have a mild case of asthma. Just a few years ago, a pulmonologist re-diagnosed my childhood respiratory condition, which I thought was in my past. Now it only shows up a couple of times a year. Typically I combat the attack with a rescue inhaler. But that inhaler proved no match for the novel coronavirus. COVID-19 laughed at the three-inch L-shaped gadget the few times I tried it days before I took myself to the hospital.

At 2:05 or 2:0-something, my mind took me to an even darker place.

Why me? Why is my life going to end this soon? What will my family do without me? How will my dear Heather hold up? How will my two teenaged sons, Ryan and Skyler, turn out after a tragedy like this? After all the hard work we put into parenting, will it all go to waste? Will they question the existence of God? Will they be angry at the world? Will they be envious of their friends who still have their fathers to teach them, to hug them, to love them?

I won't be around to see them go to college. I won't be there for their weddings. I'll never be a grandfather. I won't be able to spoil my grandkids with bits of wisdom and lots of ice cream.

Then I thought of all the things that Heather and I hoped to do once we were empty nesters. We would travel. We would do all the things we wanted to do but could never quite get to because of the day-to-day hustle and bustle of life. In my mind, those plans were gone, washed away by this poison that found its way into my bloodstream, traveling all the way from a bat cave in China.

My roommate, whom I assumed was a bit older based on the sound of his voice when he called for the nurses all through the night, was not in great shape. He was unable to control his bowels, his breathing was shallow, and his cough was dry and piercing. Whenever he coughed, I followed with one of my own. When he gasped for air, I did too.

It was the worst night of my life.

Why did I agree to spend the night in the hospital? After all, they did give me a choice.

Did that darn clock move? 2:05? 2:10? Where am I?

The banging inside my head reminded me. I was in Hell.

Then I came up with a plan. It was flawed on so many levels, but I felt like I was stuck on Groundhog Day, or Groundhog Minute. I had to do something.

I am getting out of here, jumping ship, I will escape. First, I'll take the IV out of my arm. Easy enough.

Then, I'll remove the oxygen tubes.

Wait. No, that's a bad idea.

Can I breathe without the oxygen? How will I take it with me? I'll need to confiscate a tank. Is that one in the corner, or is it a garbage can?

I was Don Quixote, jousting with windmills.

I'll make my way to the car and make a run for it, or maybe just run down the hallway. After all, I did lead the country in stolen bases.

This last bit was not a hallucination, but it was twenty-eight years ago.

I looked down at my legs. When I felt my quadriceps, there was nothing but mush—all the muscles in the front of my legs were gone. Every muscle, tendon, ligament, and bone in my body ached. I ride my bike regularly all over New York City; in fact, that's how I get to my clients. But I now had the legs of a very old man.

Reality set back in. I was stuck there for the night, watching the clock, waiting for 4 a.m. so I could take another round of Tylenol. It was now 2:11. The darn clock was not broken. I was at bat in the bottom of the ninth inning, down by a run, with two outs and two strikes against me.

Just as I was about to give up hope, I heard again the words of my living guardian angel, the shepherd of our flock who watches over me and so many others. "During challenging times, we should never feel sorry for ourselves. Jesus never felt sorry for himself."

These words rang loud and clear in my ears, but I focused my attention even more so that I could listen with the ear of my heart.

Perhaps it's part of our fallen humanity—I find it sad but true—but there are times when we need to be in darkness in order to find the light. It didn't happen for me immediately. But despite the ravages that COVID-19 wreaked on my body, my mind, and my spirit, eventually my faith, my focus, and my fitness (with the help of hydroxychloroquine) saved me.

CHAPTER TWO

BROOKLYN BEGINNINGS

My earliest memory: I'm three years old. I'm in a house with two other children. There are lots of toys, and I'm very occupied playing with them. I go into a bedroom and see my father in the bed with a woman in a black nightgown. I would love for this to be a sweet, domestic memory, one typical of my early family life. The problem—that woman was not my mother.

I found out later that he took my older siblings with him on other weekends to be with this woman and her kids. Big mistake on my father's part. John, around ten, and Janet, around nine, were old enough to know the address, and they gave it to our mom. Not a person to take his cheating lying down, Mom paid the woman a visit. She told her that the man she was sleeping with had a family he was neglecting. The woman cut off the relationship after that.

As a child, I longed to have better memories of my father. But my three older siblings and I, along with our mother, lived in constant fear whenever he was in the house.

Don't make eye contact. Maybe you'll be safe.

My oldest brother, John, told me that whenever my father left the house, he felt like he could breathe again.

Another early memory. The four of us—John, still around ten, Janet, nine, James, six, and me, three years old—were running around the apartment, acting like kids. My father had come in, but we continued playing. Out of nowhere, he grabs John, throws him against the wall, and punches a hole in it right next to his head.

"Don't you ever go past me again without stopping to say hello!"

He physically and verbally abused my mom, my siblings, and me. We had food thrown at us at the supper table, or orange juice poured over our heads because we didn't finish our breakfast.

Other times, he would come in and take off his belt. He sat on the sofa, running it through his hands, staring at us. Or he would simply set it out on the dresser for us to see. The mental terror, fearing what he might do, was worse than the actual stripes inflicted on our legs, our backs, our butts.

"I brought you into this world. I can take you out."

I'm not sure how many times I heard him say that.

Until I was almost five, we lived with my grandparents in Park Slope, Brooklyn. He couldn't keep a job. Or perhaps I should say, he wouldn't keep one. He would fly off the handle, quit, and walk out on the spot without considering that he had a wife and four children who needed to eat. Or that he should have lined up another job before quitting that one.

He cheated. He lied. And he stole—even from his family. Once, when Mom was getting ready to go out, he came into their bedroom, took her engagement and wedding rings, and went and hocked them. Debts, drugs, drink—we never learned why he would stoop so low. He openly thumbed his nose at God. Somehow, he managed to marry my mom in the church—but at the wedding rehearsal, when the priest asked him to kneel with my mom for the blessing, he said, "I kneel before no one."

I do have one fond memory of my father. I was eight or nine, and he took me with him to play racquetball. He loved the game, and he was good at it. For some reason, he picked me to go with him that weekend afternoon. We went to a deli—I ordered a spiced ham sandwich, just like he did. I picked out a mini-bottle of Canada Dry Ginger Ale from the refrigerator, and he put our lunch and drinks in a little red Igloo cooler. We walked to the park together, and we spent the rest of that afternoon hitting the ball off a concrete wall. That's it. That's my fond memory of a time with my father.

In college I studied psychology, and I learned the name for this experience—it was *a shared delight*. At least I have one. Sure, my father served as a role model—a role model for what not to do for a family. I got into arguments with professors about this—the accepted norm and wisdom from the textbooks is that abuse begets abuse. *Like father, like son.* But I made a choice to be different.

Thank God for my mother, who was our constant. Her mother was born in Ireland, her father in England. They met in the United States after my grandmother got a flat tire. She only spoke Gaelic, but as we all know, love is the universal language. They went on to have six children—three boys and three girls. Mom was fifth in the pecking order. Strong Catholics, her parents instilled in her through example and teaching the importance and strength gained through our faith.

While we lived in Park Slope, she took the four of us kids to church every Sunday at St. Thomas Aquinas. My three siblings attended school at the parish as well. All four of us have a strong faith in Jesus, despite our rough Brooklyn beginnings. We owe a debt of thanks to our mom and grandparents for bringing us up in the way we should go (Proverbs 22:6).

When we finally moved to our own apartment in Bay Ridge, we attended Our Lady of Angels, which was just across the street. I learned to play ball in that church schoolyard— stickball, softball, baseball. They may have been games for a boy, but those games eventually helped shape a man.

I loved it. I was good at it. I always played with the older kids; and if no one else was around, I would go into the school yard and throw the ball against a wall. We used cardboard boxes for bases, broom sticks for bats. If one of us could afford a real baseball and actually had a bat, we played with that ball until it fell apart. Other times we used a pink rubber ball or even a taped-up sock.

When I was nine, I played for my first organized team. A friend showed me the application to join the 68th Precinct's Police Athletic League. My father was nowhere around, but Mom scraped the money together and took me to the tryouts at a gym in Borough Park. When he saw me play, the director of the league couldn't believe that I hadn't even reached my tenth birthday. He put me in the league with the twelve-year-olds.

During that regular season, I led my team in every offensive category—batting average, RBIs, home runs, stolen bases. I started out playing center field and pitching, but I was bored in center field—not enough action. My coach, Al Humphreys, moved me to catcher, and I loved it. I was the captain in the field, controlling the game. And if the pitcher got into trouble, my catching gear came off, and I went to the mound in relief.

The season ended. I received the Sportsmanship Award—I guess I should have been happy, but I wasn't. I felt like I had taken a sucker punch to the gut. They gave the MVP Award to a twelve-year-old. He was pretty good, but I knew I was better, and I knew that everyone else knew that I was better. Evidently there was some unspoken rule that a twelve-year-old always got MVP, since they would be moving on to the next level. I would have my chance later.

The day after the award ceremony, I got a call from the butcher downstairs. He said he had a package for me. I walked into the butcher's, and I could smell the fresh cuts of meat and feel the sawdust crunching on the floor beneath my feet. On the counter above the pork sausages was a huge, oversized trophy! Inscribed on a brass plate it read—*1981 MVP Danny Venezia*. Coach Humphreys knew that justice had not been served. He went out of his way, spent his own money, to tell me that he knew who the real MVP of the team was. I can't tell you what that meant, what that still means, to a kid whose father never took him to a baseball game and had never shown up to see him play.

At least not until the next year. After another MVP regular season, I was invited to join Our Lady of Grace, a team that was going on to the ten and under playoffs. League rules allowed teams to add three players to their rosters after the regular season. We swept through the playoffs and made it to the Willie Mays Division Ten and Under World Series in Rockford, Illinois. I don't know how he did it, but somehow my father weaseled his way into serving as a chaperone for our trip.

He and I stayed in a room with another player who was added to the roster, Neil Ioviero, and his dad. That chance room assignment has turned into a lifetime friendship. He's now the head coach at Kean University in New Jersey. Neil and I talk on a regular basis about our faith, our families, our careers, and I get a morning Scripture text from him every day.

It was the last time that I had a brief glimpse of what a normal relationship might be with my father. We lost our first game in Rockford, won the second, but then lost the third game, eliminating us from the tournament. Through it all, he didn't act out or embarrass me in front of my new friend and his dad. And for those few days, ours almost felt like what a father/son relationship should be.

But after that trip, I don't remember him being around much at all. Except for one major incident.

My father was in the house and started a fight with Mom. As things continued to escalate, he picked up an alarm clock and threw it at her, barely missing hitting her in the face with it. My brother, John, was sixteen or seventeen at the time, and had grown to be a man. He confronted our father and told him to leave Mom alone.

He grabbed John by the throat.

Not a good move.

John punched him in the mouth, knocking out a couple of front teeth. That was the end of the fight, but my father got in the last word.

"If you ever raise your hands to me again, I'll kill you."

It wasn't the first time that John was called on to be the man in our family. At ten, he worked a paper route and gave half of the money he earned to Mom for groceries. He did that until he was twelve, when he got a job in a delicatessen making more money. As the oldest, a lot of responsibility fell heavily on his pre-teen shoulders.

The year I graduated from elementary school, James graduated from junior high, and Janet graduated from high school. My father didn't show up for any of those events. During that summer, our rent didn't get paid. As fall approached, Mom had to make a very difficult decision. We were kicked out of our apartment, and to keep our family together, she had to split us up.

We all stayed with different family members. James and I went to my Aunt Jeannie and Uncle George's on Long Island. It was only for a couple months, but it was life changing for me.

Every night, and I mean every night, we would sit down at the supper table and have a family meal together—my aunt and uncle, my cousins Ronnie and Jeannie, James, and me. We talked, we laughed, we actually enjoyed one another's company! No raging, no threats, no food thrown or drinks poured over anyone's head. As heartwarming as that was, it was what happened just as we sat down to eat that has stayed with me ever since.

Before anyone lifted a fork, we took turns saying a blessing over our meal. I couldn't wait until it was my turn every six days. My family today still uses this prayer:

Thank you, dear Lord, for this food we're about to receive.
Thank you for all the blessings you've given us. Help
anyone who needs our prayers.

Those three simple sentences taught me so much about life, so much about faith. First, to be thankful for our food. That was foreign to me in our family life. We were always in survival mode. But to stop, to reflect, to realize that God above had provided this meal for our nourishment—it made a lifetime impression on me.

Second, to be thankful for other blessings. Up to that point in my life, I had never really thought about being thankful for anything. In fact, in my mind, I was probably cursing God—I didn't think my prayers were ever answered.

Why didn't I get a new baseball glove like so-and-so? Or new sneakers? Why do I get the hand-me-down clothes from my brothers? Why didn't my father come home at night, or ever take me to a baseball game, or ever come to mine?

This simple prayer opened my spirit to focus on the things in my life that I could be thankful for—my brothers and my sister, my incredible mom, and my God-given physical abilities as an athlete.

Third, I learned to pray for others. My faith life, as budding and nascent as it was, was all about me. This third sentence not only made me aware that I should be praying for others, but also that others were likely praying for me!

Those months with my aunt and uncle were my first experience with normalcy. I longed for a place of trust, encouragement, faith. Today, that family remains strong in their faith, and my cousins' families are strong Christians as well. In that home, I learned a lot about what I wanted in life and what I hoped for in a family.

While we were separated, Mom took the bull by the horns. She focused her energies, worked on her typing skills, and landed a good paying job at Chemical Bank. She rented an apartment for the five of us in Bensonhurst—my father was no longer welcome in our home. Our residence may have been filled with roaches, but it was no longer filled with hatred.

I started junior high that year and quickly became friends with Joe Fuccillo. We have been best friends ever since. Like me, Joe spent time as a professional baseball player and is now a fitness trainer. During my days in the hospital, he was constantly sending me text messages of encouragement.

You're one of the toughest guys I know. You will beat this!

Joe's mom and dad became like my second parents. Suppertime at Joe's house was like being back at my aunt and uncle's—his family sat down at the table for meals every night. After an afternoon of stickball, baseball, or softball, I often joined them for dinner. Even then I believe that my wounded heart was healing from the screaming, the food being thrown, the living in fear of what might erupt at any moment.

But trust me, I wasn't getting soft. Growing up in Brooklyn, you either got tough or you were eaten alive. Bensonhurst wasn't Brooklyn's toughest neighborhood, but it was still pretty rough. When I was thirteen and walking home from school one day, I came upon four punks around my age, picking on a little guy. Not just picking on—beating him up, rifling through his school bag, pocketing what they wanted and destroying the rest. Every time the kid would try to get his bag, they would kick, slap, or punch him. Three of them were doing all of the dirty work—the fourth, smaller and Asian, just seemed to be along for the ride. But he certainly wasn't doing anything to stop it. I decided I should.

"Why don't you give him his things and pick on someone who'll hit you back? I have better stuff in my bag."

That got their attention away from him. Now they focused on me.

"Oh. So the new kid on the block is a tough guy," one of them said.

The boy they were picking on got what was left of his belongings and headed in the opposite direction.

As they surrounded me, I realized that two of them looked identical. Twins. Tall, lanky, black hair slicked back against their heads—definitely Italian toughs. The third punk was the loudest and did most of the hitting and kicking. He was stockier than the twins, and his black hair was buzzed with a crew cut.

I took stock of my situation, which wasn't too good. I wasn't worried about the Asian kid, but the other three would be a challenge. I mainly wanted one good shot at Mr. Big Mouth—I figured if I took the leader down, I might knock the fight out of the other two as well. I probably could have outrun them—I was always the fastest on my baseball teams—but spending the rest of the school year looking over my shoulder to see if they were coming after me didn't sit right.

"I'll take you on, one at a time. Who's first?"

It was worth a try. But it failed miserably.

First, the twins jumped me from behind and held me down. I couldn't get one good swing in. Mr. Big Mouth punched and kicked me, and the other two got in their licks as they could. My face was down in the cement of the sidewalk—it protected me from too much damage. In my peripheral vision I could see Mr. Big Mouth's sneakers going back and forth as he kicked me—white Adidas with blue stripes. I started seeing red on them, which wasn't there before. It was my blood.

They destroyed the few books that were in my book bag and took three dollars out of my pocket. I had been on the way to the corner store to get bread and milk. I got home, cleaned myself up before anyone saw me, and told no one about what happened. I told Mom I had lost the three dollars. But I had a plan.

Wearing a pair of shades and a baseball cap, I followed them to their apartment and cased the joint. As it turned out, these three were not only brothers, they were triplets. The "twins" were identical, and Mr. Big Mouth was fraternal. My plan was to catch them alone, one at a time, and wreak my revenge. But as triplets, they were almost always together. They lived just down the street from me, on the other side of 14th Avenue. From my window, I could monitor their coming and going.

A week later, during a stakeout around 6 p.m., one of the twins left the apartment alone and started walking down the street, toward my apartment. I raced outside and followed him down the sidewalk. I finally caught up, tapped him on the shoulder, and caught him with a right cross to his glass chin. He went down, and I came down on top of him, raining several more blows for good measure. All he did was try to cover his face.

It was my lucky day. On my way back to my apartment, unlucky twin number two comes out of the candy store. My adrenaline was pumping. I wrestled him to the sidewalk and pulled eight dollars out of his pocket.

"Tell your brother he's next."

I went home and gave Mom the three dollars I had lost. She asked no questions, and I gave her no answers.

The very next day I ran into the Asian kid in the bathroom at school. I grabbed him by the hair. Tears ran down his face, and he did go to the bathroom—he just never made it to the urinal.

"I'm not going to hit you," I said. "But be sure and tell your friends—that guy you messed with, if you come near him again, you won't get off so easy."

He thanked me in broken English through his tears. No punches necessary, and the score was now Good Guy 3, Bad Guys 0 (I figured the first one didn't count in the standings because it was an unfair contest—four against one).

It was a week later before the last of the triplets gave me the opportunity to catch him alone. He rarely left his apartment without a gang of thugs around him, and if he did, he would sprint past my apartment. Fear can be quite a motivator to action.

Finally, one rainy day, I saw him leave the apartment by himself. He started running, and I sprinted outside to catch him. It took me five blocks, but eventually he ran out of gas. He stopped behind a 1979 Chevy and leaned against the trunk, trying to catch his breath. When I caught up to him, he started circling the car.

"Please don't hit me. Please don't hit me!" he begged. "We want to be friends with you."

I didn't hit him. And eventually we became acquaintances, if not friends. My vigilante days were over.

Just as we had in Park Slope and Bay Ridge, Mom saw to it that we attended the local parish church in Bensonhurst, The Basilica of Regina Pacis. Eventually I was confirmed there. But, like too many teenagers, my faith waned during those years. Hanging out with Mr. Big Mouth and his brothers and friends didn't help.

I do remember one answered prayer from around that time. Puberty came really late for me. At thirteen, I was shorter than everyone else in my class. With my new "friends," I had picked up the habit of smoking. One day, I made a deal with God.

"Dear Lord," I prayed, "make me grow, and I'll never smoke again."

I kept my side of the bargain, and God kept his! I grew six inches that year. Later, when I was in college, I was out drinking with the fellas one night. I lit a cigarette. After a couple of puffs, I felt the sickest I had ever felt (until COVID-19). I *really* never smoked again after that.

I never got into any real serious trouble in my Bensonhurst days, but I certainly could have headed down that path, especially considering the crowd I was hanging out with.

One day, my buddies and I were out on our block. Mr. Romano was a next-door neighbor. He had come to America from Italy, and he loved to sit outside his apartment in an old 1950's kitchenette chair, playing his accordion. It wasn't the coolest music for young teenagers in the mid-1980s, and my friends made fun of him. Not only that, but he had polio. His left arm was shriveled into an unnatural position, but one that perfectly suited his accordion playing.

He stopped playing that day and called me over.

"Danny boy, show me your friends…"

I started to point them out across the street. Before I could, he stopped me with his good hand, then continued.

"…show me your friends, and I'll show you who you are."

In that moment, I had an out-of-body experience. I looked down at myself, and I looked across the street at my "friends." I was not who I wanted to be. *They* were not who I wanted to be.

One of them was writing graffiti on a door. Another was drinking a beer out of a paper bag.

"Yes, Mr. Romano," was all I said.

In that moment, I chose to be a different person.

Instead of spending time on the corner, I spent time on the diamond.

Instead of throwing punches, I threw a baseball.

Instead of stealing cars, I stole bases.

I can tell you stories about those very kids on that corner that day. All of them wound up doing drugs. One went away to prison for a long time. One was killed in a drive-by shooting. And another killed himself playing Russian roulette. The story I heard was that he had taken the clip out of the automatic pistol but didn't realize there was already a bullet in the chamber. Whether or not that's what happened, or if it was a cover-up for something more nefarious, we will probably never know.

There was trouble in that neighborhood if you wanted it. I chose not to want it.

God sent his guardian angels around me in my Brooklyn years: Coach Humphreys, Mr. Romano, Coach Gavigan—he was an NYC police officer, and he took me with his family to my first Yankee game.

Then there's Sal Cappucci. Mr. Cappucci taught my siblings and me eighth grade science. He also coached baseball in the summer. He would take some of us to dinner, he took us skiing, he even took another kid and me to Disney World. Mr. Cappucci played a significant role in my life throughout my high school years. Before I could drive, he would pick me up in his car and drive me to games when Mom was working and unavailable. He bought me a new baseball glove when I needed it, and he coached my team that went to the National Amateur Baseball Federation World Series in 1986.

He taught me to drive, and then he sold me my first car—a blue 1981 Mercury Cougar. I had worked for two years delivering papers and saved $2,000 to purchase the car.

My sophomore year in high school, I made the varsity baseball team at Fort Hamilton High. We were terrible. I think we were 1 and 13 for the season. Our field was in even worse shape than our team. At the time, I was maybe five and a half feet tall and a little over a hundred pounds soaking wet—I was in college before I finally grew to my height of 6'1"—so I always played second base through those years. After numerous grounders found the dips and crevices and rocks in the infield, taking bad hops past me, I decided to do something about it.

I borrowed a pair of heavy-duty bolt cutters from the school and went to a local park where there was a long chain link fence. It was a public park, right? The public owned it. I'm part of that public, and I needed a section of that fence. No, *my team* needed a section of that fence.

I cut out a piece large enough to fold in half and still be the width of the trunk of my Cougar. I put weights on it, tied it with rope, held it in place by closing my trunk on the rope, and used it to rake our awful infield, just like I had seen professional groundskeepers do. I drove my car onto the field and started around the pitcher's mound, driving in circles until I had smoothed out the entire infield area.

My high school coach, Jim Apicella, never asked where I got the chain link fence. But he and the rest of my team appreciated my going the extra mile.

My junior year, we fared better, winning about half of our games. I was named captain that year. It was my senior year, though, that became something special. As I said earlier, I was the smallest kid on the team. Everyone else was bigger, stronger, and many were more talented. But no one worked harder than I did. I was always willing to do whatever it took to be my best, and I never even settled for that. I wanted to be better than my best. My pent-up anger at my dad was unleashed when I hit a baseball—I saw his face on it as it left the pitcher's hand.

That senior year, we went 17 and 2 in the regular season. I was named to the All-City team as a second baseman, and one paper named our school the number one team in New York City. I didn't have the highest batting average, by any means, but I excelled on defense; and on offense, I bunted to get on base, I moved runners into scoring position, and I led my team in stolen bases.

We were one of thirty-two teams that reached the playoffs for the City Championship. We swept through our first four games to make it to the championship game, which was to be held in Yankee Stadium. Lincoln High, Fort Hamilton's rival and one of the schools that beat us in the regular season, was to be our opponent.

The day of the final game, it poured rain. The game was postponed and rescheduled for a few days later at St. John's University. We were bitterly disappointed. Sure, St. John's had a nice facility, but it was no Yankee Stadium!

My co-captain, Jermaine Swinton (who was 6'4", 220 pounds—at sixteen-years-old a true man-child who was drafted a few days earlier by the Houston Astros), and I were at Coach Apicella's house the next day, bemoaning the loss of getting to play in Yankee Stadium. On a whim, we decided to call in to WFAN-AM, New York City's talk radio sports station. We told our sob story, and a great thing happened. Someone from the radio station called George Steinbrenner, the owner of the Yankees, and told him our story. He made some calls and arranged for us to play our game in Yankee Stadium a few days later.

It was one of the greatest days of my life. To walk out on that field, in the House that Ruth Built, where Lou Gehrig, Joe DiMaggio, Mickey Mantle, and countless other Hall of Famers had played the game that I was about to play, was every kid who loves baseball's dream. In the bottom of the third, I reached base on an error, was awarded second on the shortstop's bad throw, and scored our team's first run when Coach Apicella waved me home on a single to left by my double play partner, Julius Alphonso.

We went on to win the game, 10 to 4. I assisted on the final play to secure the win, fielding a sharp grounder to my left and throwing the runner out. Ending with a record of 22-2, it was the first City Championship in our school's history. I was in heaven! The next day, Mayor Ed Koch gave us the key to the city. I believed I owned it.

That summer after my senior year, I played in the Youth Service League, which was started to get youth in rough neighborhoods off the streets of New York in the summer. The tryouts for the team had started the winter before. Coach Mel ran the tryouts, and he was a drill sergeant. In all of my career as a professional baseball player and as a fitness trainer myself, I was never worked as hard as I was by him. For ten straight Saturdays we took batting practice, fielded grounders, and ran until we threw up. Literally.

I left there with bruises on my legs and chest from the scorching grounders he hit at me. I woke Sunday mornings with cramps in my hamstrings. It was brutal. But it was effective. He took tough kids and made us tougher.

College coaches and big league scouts knew of Mel's reputation, and they would come to watch his tryouts. Three of my teammates—Manny Ramirez, Frank Rodriguez, and José Flores—made it to the majors. Several more of us were selected in the MLB draft.

From those tryouts, I got two college offers. Brooklyn College, a Division I school, offered me a scholarship. I could basically stay at home and play some big-time NYC baseball. The other offer came from a Division II school, about an hour out of the city: Concordia College, a small Lutheran school in Bronxville, New York.

My brother-in-law at the time, Jamie, said to me, "Danny, Brooklyn will be here when you come back. But you need to go away."

I called Carmine DiGrande, one of the coaches who recruited me to Concordia, and told him I wanted to come to Bronxville.

As I look back on my eighteen years in Brooklyn, I see the importance, the significance, of the little moments that shape a life:

Coach Humphreys buying me that trophy.

Aunt Jeannie and Uncle George teaching me a simple pre-meal blessing.

Mr. Romano's comment about my friends.

Jamie telling me to get away from Brooklyn.

My life there was coming to an end. I escaped the trouble, the hopelessness that engulfs far too many in urban America. That summer, my team went on to the Connie Mack World Series in Farmington, New Mexico. That fall, I left to begin my college career.

CHAPTER THREE

NOTHING GOOD COMES EASY

"Thank you for coming in, Dan. We need to talk about your grades."

It's almost never a good thing to get called into the dean's office. That certainly was true for me that late spring morning of my freshman year.

We were nearing the end of my first year playing college ball. I had started out on the bench during the fall season, typical for most freshmen—and I hated it. I eventually got onto the field at second base, but I knew that if I wanted to keep my position, I had to work harder than everyone else.

When I started college, I had grown to 5'10" from being only 5' my freshman year of high school, but I still weighed just 150 pounds on a good day. I needed to be stronger, and I knew I needed to be bigger to get to where I wanted to be. During that winter, I went to work on my body. I worked out religiously, doing five sets of one hundred push-ups every other day, five sets of two hundred sit-ups on the off days. I held my nose and drank two nasty tasting Nutrament shakes every day, at 360 calories each. I lifted weights, did calisthenics, and I ate everything I could get my hands on. By the start of the spring baseball season, I had grown three inches in height and put on thirty-five pounds of muscle.

And I played well. I hit .350 in the spring, not too shabby for a freshman. Our team did even better—we led the nation among Division II schools with a team batting average of .391. I was doing what I loved with a bunch of guys that really enjoyed one another's company. Concordia College only had four hundred students, most of whom were religion or music majors. As athletes, we were very different from the average, and as members of the baseball team, we really stood out. There was one dining hall for the entire school, and at its very center was "The Round Table." All the other tables in the room were square. The baseball team claimed the round table as its own, and no one else dared to inhabit it. The cocky athletes that we were, we considered the other students as square as the tables they sat at. Now, as I look back on those days, I can only wish that I had gotten to know and appreciate those "squares."

Being only an hour away from home, I was able to visit my family on a number of weekends. What could have gone better my freshman year? One major thing—I was a college *student*, and I left out a major component of fulfilling that role—*studying*.

Not only that, but being a Lutheran college, Concordia had required religion courses for underclassmen. My first semester, that religion class started at 7:50 a.m. I never made it, not ever. Somehow, only God knows how, I passed that course with a D. Unfortunately, I didn't fare so well in my English class, which was later in the afternoon. Not being a baseball fan, the female professor didn't understand why I chose to go to baseball practice or one of our games over attending her class. I got a well-deserved F in that course.

By now, you're getting the picture. I did an excellent job of focusing my energy and time on my fitness and ball playing. But I was way below average in my performance as a student. My GPA of 1.7 that second semester attracted the attention of the dean and got me called into his office.

"I understand our baseball team, and you included, are having a pretty good season," he began.

"Yes, sir," I said.

I appreciated his nod to my baseball play.

"But, Dan, you understand that there's much more to being a student at Concordia than playing baseball."

"Sure, sir. I —"

"Let me finish, son. Your grades are not meeting the standard we expect—no, we require—of our student athletes. I have to put you on probation. If you don't get your grades up next semester, you will lose your scholarship, and you will be in jeopardy of not being allowed to stay at Concordia."

This was cold water in my face. My life goal was to make it to the big leagues as a baseball player, but the first step toward doing that was to have a successful career as a college player. And now I had to face the reality of what it meant to be a student athlete.

My sophomore year, I applied the same focus and dedication to my studies that I had previously used on my fitness and skills for baseball. My grades improved. I had a 3.5 GPA that fall semester, and I never dropped below that the rest of my time in college. I made the Dean's List six straight semesters—much better than being called to his office. By the time of my first semester senior year, I pulled down a 4.0.

That fall baseball season, I came to appreciate what I had as a student playing baseball at Concordia. The campus, and especially the area around the baseball field, was beautiful as the leaves on the great oak trees that hung over the field in places turned a kaleidoscope of colors.

Looking back, I see the challenges we faced playing on that field. While the fence down the right field foul line was only 289 feet away, it was deceptively difficult to get the ball over it. We literally did not have a level playing field. To get to that right field corner, you had to climb a small hill; and for the right fielder, that meant avoiding a rather large rock that stuck up out of the grass.

Even in the dugout, we had to play heads up baseball. Both dugouts were only fifteen feet from home plate—a line drive foul ball could leave more than a mark if you weren't paying attention. Left fielders had to be fearless in going after balls down the line. The brick wall of the athletic center was two feet outside of that foul line. A lot of pop flies dropped in as singles because of players unwilling to challenge that wall.

While I managed to survive the academic struggles I faced my freshman year, I disappointed myself by going along with the crowd during my second semester sophomore year.

Coach Carmine DiGrande and Head Coach Lou Santos had been good to me from the moment I was recruited—especially Coach Carmine. But at the end of that sophomore year, a number of players were unhappy and circulated a petition to have them both replaced. Succumbing to peer pressure, I signed it. Later, as I thought about it, I realized it was primarily the guys who didn't perform, who didn't put in the work, who were disgruntled. Almost immediately, I regretted doing it.

These two men took a chance on a small kid from Brooklyn. They believed in me, gave me a great opportunity, and I felt like

I had betrayed their trust. The only thing I could think to do was to call them both and tell them what I had done and that I was sorry for it.

They were both incredibly gracious to an immature kid who should have done better. Rather than holding a grudge, each of them said they were happy to hear from me and wished me well in my career. I'll never forget Coach Carmine's words:

"It's water under the bridge."

I believe I became a man that day when I picked up the phone and made those calls. I owned up to a flaw in my character, a weakness that had been exposed when I allowed the crowd to influence me into doing something that I knew in my heart was wrong. Yet another tough lesson.

Two years later, we lost another coach and a man who had a profound influence on me—Harry Tanney. This was a man who you would have thought never had a bad day, never met a person he didn't like, who always managed to walk down the sunny side of the street. I was devastated when I learned he passed away. His words encouraged me when I was in the hospital with COVID-19, struggling to get out of the bed and walk to the window and back:

"Always give one hundred percent."

I know, that sounds so simple, and we've heard it a million times; but when Harry said it to me, it stuck. And it reverberated off those hospital walls when I needed it the most.

A few months before he passed away that spring, he called me after I had a particularly bad game at shortstop. I mean bad—I made three errors in one inning. He called to tell me about another player who had played short at Concordia—Scott Leuis, who was playing for the Minnesota Twins at that time.

"Danny, don't you dare let today get to you. Scott didn't when he had a day like yours. In fact, it fueled him to get better. You know what he did?"

"What, Coach?"

"For the rest of that season, he showed up at 8 a.m. to field grounders before class. He never had a day like that again."

I took Harry's advice. I took it to the next level. Michael Roig, a workout geek like me, was my partner. Every morning we were up at 5:30 a.m. Remember, this is in the Northeast. We weren't in Florida, Arizona, or California where you could train outside year 'round.

So we went into the tennis center on campus where we stored a portable batting cage. The whole athletic department shared this facility, so we had to put the cage together every morning and tear it back down when we were done. It took us thirty minutes just to set it up. But once we did, we would throw a bucket of balls to each other for batting practice. Then we would hit dozens of grounders to each other to improve our fielding. Last, we ran with the Danny Venezia power harness.

My entire career, I was always working on gadgets to help improve my game. I had seen something similar advertised in a magazine for eighty bucks. Not having that kind of cash as a student, I figured I could make something like it that would accomplish the same thing.

I tied a rubber jump rope to a weight belt and secured it with a plastic tube. It looked like a waterskiing rope. Each of us would put on the belt and try to run sprints, with the other person holding us back by the rope. I became quicker, more explosive out of the batter's box and off the bases. I was already fast around the bases—now I could get up to my maximum speed much faster. My junior year, I led the nation among all NCAA Division II schools in stolen bases. It must have been working.

In November of my senior year, I celebrated my twenty-first birthday by drinking one beer. I decided that I would drink no more alcohol that school year. I was determined to do everything I could to give myself the best chance of getting drafted to play professional baseball.

Throughout my first three years at Concordia, I had alternated in the infield between shortstop and second. I asked my coach to let me stay at short that senior season. I knew that second basemen rarely get drafted. Scouts want to know that you have the arm strength, the mental capacity, and the soft hands needed to play shortstop. Coach agreed.

That year, in thirty games I hit .464 with six homers, twelve doubles, twenty-four RBIs, a slugging percentage of .855, and I only struck out twice. I also stole twenty-four bases and only had two errors at short. Numbers can be impressive, but they aren't everything, and they certainly aren't a guarantee of attracting a major league team to draft you.

I stayed up late at night to write letters to every major league team's front office and scouting department and sent several to the Major League Scouting Bureau. I wanted them to know that I was hungry, I was going for it.

Late in that season, as we were warming up for a game, I spotted Herb Stein, one of the game's most respected scouts, walking down the side of the field. He had on a fishing cap and carried a briefcase with a big "Minnesota Twins" emblem on it. Just before I saw him, I had the worst batting practice, ever. I ran in from short for another round of BP—I wasn't sure if he had seen the previous one or not. I knew this could be my one big opportunity, and I wasn't going to let it go to waste.

I felt like God was really looking out for me at that moment. After just having my worst, I then had one of my best rounds of hitting ever. I hit everything hard. I hit four home runs in a row, with six or seven in the round. After the last one sailed deep over the left field fence, I walked back toward the dugout.

"Hey, Danny." Herb called me over.

"It's a pleasure to meet you, sir," I said, my adrenaline pumping.

After he got my address and phone number, he asked, "Danny, what is your outlook on life?"

All I could think of was the current marketing slogan that Reebok was using.

"Life is short. Play hard," I said.

He laughed.

"Well, son, I'm seventy-six years old. Life isn't so short."

I laughed with him. And that was our only interaction.

During the game, my first at bat I popped up to the first baseman. But I used everything I had trained for, including the Danny Venezia power harness, to explode out of the batter's box and sprint to first base. I figured he had a stopwatch on me. I wanted him to know that I was a hustler—that I would run everything out.

Second time up, I heard the sounds I love—first the crack of the bat and then the leaves rustling in those great oaks outside the left-center field fence. The ball whisked its way through them. A home run. As I rounded second, I looked up to see Herb's reaction. He was no longer sitting where he had been—he had picked up his chair and was walking back to the parking lot.

In that moment, I knew I had a shot. He had seen what he needed to see in me as a player. I'm sure he talked to my coach and knew about my daily 5:30 a.m. workout routine. He had read my hungry letter. I had the focus needed to be a major league baseball player. And I had the work ethic and natural God-given athletic ability to make it worth giving me a chance.

I didn't drop the ball with my baseball playing, but I did with my academics during my last semester.

I was doing great! As I mentioned earlier, I had really turned my academics around by applying myself, working harder than anyone else, and staying focused on the goal until I reached it and surpassed it. My senior year I was given the Mickey Byrne Scholar Athlete Award, the school's highest honor, given to the top student athlete (all sports included). But that last spring, I let up, coasted toward the end of the semester, and got a couple of Bs instead of straight As.

At the commencement ceremony, while many of my friends received the honor of *summa cum laude*, *magna cum laude*, or *cum laude*, I simply graduated. I missed the distinction by hundredths of a grade point—I finished with a 3.4 something. Just one more A, just one more class focused on until I crossed home plate, and I would have reached my goal.

Sure, in the grand scheme of things, it might not matter that much whether or not I graduated with honors. But I knew in my heart that I could have done better. If I had applied myself, if I had just worked a little bit harder, my name would have been called out on that list. And it was my fault that it wasn't. A hard lesson, but one I determined then and there that I would never have to learn again.

CHAPTER FOUR

EVERY BOY'S DREAM

The phone rang. My heart dropped. I picked up the phone. "Hey, Danny, any news yet?"

It was my friend, Anthony Leone. Like me, he was hoping to get that once in a lifetime call as well. The fulfillment of our boyhood dreams—playing in the big leagues—was now dependent on one phone call. This one wasn't it.

Just the week before, I had heard from the California Angels. They asked if I would sign a professional contract, how much it would take for me to sign, and to fill out a health form. That sounded hopeful, right? Maybe they would call. I had told them that yes, I absolutely would sign a professional contract, and that I would accept whatever they thought appropriate for where they drafted me. I was in great health—no major injuries like many other players have to deal with in their amateur careers.

Just call me! I wanted to scream into the phone.

I had been sitting around the house all day, hoping and praying for that one call. I hung up from talking to Anthony and decided I had to get out of the apartment. I was helpless—for the first time in my life, I had no control over my baseball career. No extra swings in the batting cage, no extra ground balls at 5:30 in the morning, no running in my homemade power harness was going to make that phone ring with the right person on the other end. The waiting, the anticipation, the fear of disappointment was getting to be too much. I needed fresh air, I needed a fresh perspective, and Mom needed some fresh mozzarella.

It was now 4:30 in the afternoon. Getting late. Of course, there could be a third day of later round drafts. Maybe the phone would ring tomorrow.

So off to the store I went.

As I walked down the block, I felt like I had those two cartoon characters on each of my shoulders. The little angel in white was whispering words of encouragement. "Don't worry, Danny. You'll be rewarded for all your hard work."

Dressed in red, his pitchfork poking into my brain, a little demon argued the other side. "That's just a dream, Danny Boy. Wake up to reality. Do you know the odds of getting drafted? You might as well head over to the OTB—you'll have better luck at the racetrack."

I started thinking the unthinkable. What if baseball wasn't in my future? I had no backup, no Plan B. Sure, I had majored in psychology in college, and I completed my degree in four years. But I had no burning desire to go any further in that field.

"Don't worry, Danny. You've always known what you wanted to do. Follow your heart. Your dreams will come true."

The angel got in the last word as I walked into the store. I headed for aisle eight, where I knew I would find the mozzarella, when I felt a tap on my shoulder. I turned around to see my girlfriend at the time with a big smile on her face. There could be only one reason for that smile.

Right there in aisle eight, beside the cheese display, we displayed our joy at a young boy's dream coming true. I even screamed.

"I'm a professional baseball player!"

We laughed and ran out of the store, the shopping forgotten. And then it hit me.

"Who called?" I asked.

"Herb Stein."

I knew then that I was part of the Minnesota Twins organization, joining my Concordia teammate and close friend, Butch Burrough, who was drafted the year before.

"He said for you to call as soon as possible."

We ran all the way home. I walked into our apartment, completely out of breath, and was greeted by my Mom's proud, beaming face. Seeing the joy my success brought her made all the hard work, all the focus and self-discipline I had learned from her example, worth every moment of it.

A few more hugs, lots of laughter, and maybe a few tears, and I went to the phone to return Herb's call. He was warm, encouraging, and assured me that he believed in me and thought I would have a very successful professional career.

Just after our conversation ended, the following letter arrived special delivery:

June 4, 1993

Dear Daniel:

The Minnesota Twins are pleased to inform you that we have selected you in the 1993 Free Agent Draft.

It is a great honor to be selected for a career in Professional Baseball, and it is a tribute to your abilities, hard work, and dedication to the game. We have followed your career at Concordia College, and we hope you are interested in a Professional Baseball career. You will be contacted shortly by our scout, Herb Stein, who will handle contract negotiations.

Again, congratulations on your selection, and we look forward to having you join the TWINS Organization.

Sincerely,
Larry Corrigan,
Director of Scouting

Herb came to our house with the contract. He looked embarrassed, and he apologized when he told me that my signing bonus was only a thousand dollars. I didn't tell him this, but I would have paid *him* a thousand dollars to sign that contract and become a professional baseball player.

He told us stories of other players he had signed in his forty years with the Twins. Scott Leuis, who also played shortstop at Concordia, hit a game winning home run in game two of the 1991 World Series. Gene Larkin had the game winning hit in game seven of the '87 World Series. From that same series, he had signed pitcher Frank Viola, who was named MVP and went on to win the Cy Young Award that year. But Herb's biggest signing was Rod Carew, a Hall of Famer whose name always comes up when people argue about the greatest hitters in baseball history. When Herb took off his two World Series rings and let me hold them, I felt like I had the world's most precious jewels in my hands.

Needless to say, I signed the contract, and we shook hands on the deal. Two days later, I said goodbye to my family, goodbye to Brooklyn, got on an airplane at LaGuardia, and headed to Fort Myers, Florida for the Twins' rookie mini-camp.

That night I met my roommate, Chad Rupp. Chad had played at the University of Miami, one of the top baseball schools in the nation. At 6'2" and 210 pounds, he was a big, strong first baseman who could hit the ball a country mile. The next morning we got up early to go to the Twins' Class A team's facility where our practices were held.

I had never been in a clubhouse that big. Starstruck just being there, I looked and saw VENEZIA in big bold letters above the locker right next to the showers. Hanging there was a Twins' jersey with the number "23" on the back, along with a pair of navy-blue pinstriped baseball pants. Bursting with pride and joy, I put on my uniform and Twins cap, and I went out to the batting cage to hit with Chad.

That evening we decided to celebrate before our first inter-squad game the next day. We went to a place called Hooters—the wings were hot, the beer was cold, and the service was even better. The two of us went through several pitchers of beer before we got home in the wee hours of the morning.

Needless to say, I wasn't in the best shape for my first professional competition just a few hours later. The game started before noon. The first pitcher I faced, Tommy Gourdin, had a ninety-plus mph fastball. It might as well have been a hundred and ninety to my glazed eyes. On top of that, there weren't many pitchers who could deliver that kind of heat in Division II ball. So even on a good day, it would have been difficult for me. I struck out on four pitches. Later, I found out this guy was a converted catcher.

Holy crap. Can I do this? I thought.

I knew then I couldn't party with the boys at night if I wanted to perform on the diamond in the daytime.

I spent extra time in the batting cage before practice and games, cranking up the speed on the JUGS pitching machine to try and get my eye trained to pick up faster balls. I'm not sure how many total at bats I had during mini-camp, but I do know how many hits I had—just one. I felt like I had gotten a piano off of my back when I made solid contact and saw the ball go through the middle of the infield.

At the beginning of mini-camp, I experienced my first doubts as to whether or not I belonged there. I was constantly comparing myself to the other players—where they went to school, what round they were drafted in, who had gotten a $100,000 signing bonus. Could I really compete with that level of competition? After that first hit, I was able to recapture my positive outlook.

A few days later, a number of us were on our way to Elizabethton, Tennessee, to the Twins' advanced rookie team. We left Fort Myers at 6 a.m. for a very long bus ride. To pass the time, we played cards.

We had been playing for a buck or two a hand, and I had been winning pretty handily. One of the guys, Tom Knauss, wanted to raise the stakes to ten bucks a hand, which was a bit rich for my blood. He was younger, drafted in the second-round right out of high school and received a much higher signing bonus than I did. I was ready to go to the back of the bus and take a nap, especially since I was well ahead, but he kept after me to play another hand.

"How much cash do you have?" I asked.

He pulled eighty dollars out of his wallet. I matched it.

"Let's draw cards. High card takes it all. Win or lose, I'm going to sleep after this."

When he drew a queen, he went nuts. You would have thought he'd just won the World Series (I did the numbers quickly in my head). Only eight of the fifty-one cards left in the deck would beat him. That's not a very good chance of victory. But something told me, down deep in my knower, that I was not going to lose—maybe because I was a bit older or a bit wiser, maybe because I saw a little of myself in him. I had been in situations like this before and was set straight by someone older.

I drew my card. Without even looking at it myself, I showed it to him and the other guys on the bus, who had gathered around to see what happened. Their faces told me what I needed to know. I tossed the King of Hearts on top of the deck, gathered my $160, and got up to take my nap.

I'm not sure what the kid thought of me in that moment, but I could tell that I had gained a lot of respect from the other fellas with the way I dealt with the situation. He and I would soon do battle together as teammates and eventually become friends.

There's nothing very glamorous about life in baseball's rookie league. Long bus rides, cramped motel rooms, and fifteen dollars a day for meals are my main memories from those months. We played in the Appalachian League—Huntington, Virginia; Burlington, North Carolina; Kingsport, Tennessee; and Princeton, West Virginia feel like a long, long way from Brooklyn, New York.

Scott Stricklin joined Chad and me as a roommate that year. Scott is now the head coach of the Georgia Bulldogs in the SEC. With our fifteen dollar a day food allowance, the three of us would often sleep in and skip breakfast, pick up fast food for lunch, and then try to find a restaurant for a decent meal at dinner time. Most days we had to tap into our salary money, $850 a month before taxes, to get that good meal. Other guys chose Taco Bell three times a day to stay within their food allowance budget. Even at twenty-one years old, I thought more of my body than that.

My best friend, Joe, was signed by the Cincinnati Reds. He had gone to a tryout and blew them away with his fastball. Assigned to their rookie team in the same league, we eventually faced each other that year.

As I stepped into the batter's box, I tried not to look him in the eye. It was hard—I wanted to do well. Every time I went to the plate, I felt like I needed to prove to the Twins that I belonged in professional baseball. At the same time, I was pulling for my friend to succeed as well. He must have been feeling the same way. That first time up against Joe, he walked me on four straight pitches. I've never let him live that down.

All in all, I had a really good rookie year. In sixty games, I had eighty hits, batted .310 to lead my team as the leadoff batter, and stole twenty-one bases, also best on the team and best in the league. My focus throughout that time was to be selected for the fall Instructional League. This was for the top prospects in the organization—those believed to have a legitimate shot at making the big time. Only thirty of the two hundred players throughout the Twins' organization would be chosen. With a week remaining in our rookie schedule, our manager, Ray Smith, approached me.

"Hey, Danny. Whatcha' doin' when the season's over?"

"Why, Ray?"

I didn't want to get too excited.

"Wanna play some more baseball in the fall?"

"Yes, sir! You bet I do!"

My dream was coming true. I went home to Brooklyn for about two weeks and then headed back to Fort Myers, Florida, where the Twins had their winter headquarters and ran their Instructional League. The Instructional League was just that—instructions on the fundamentals of baseball. You might have all the talent in the world, but if your mechanics were sloppy fielding a ground ball, turning a double play, or moving a runner over into scoring position, your talent might not take you all the way to the Show.

Up at 7 a.m. every morning, six days a week for seven weeks, the mornings were spent practicing those fundamentals. We used the same signs and ran the same plays that the Twins major league team used. That way, if you got called up, you were prepared to fit right in. I'm sure they must have kept statistics on us, but they never told us what they were. They cared more about seeing us improve in our individual skills than our stats.

The Fort Myers facility was the one the Twins used for their spring training. For that reason, the clubhouse and locker room were big league all the way—aerobic machines, weights, training staff. The field we practiced and played on was pristine. After lunch every day, we played a game—sometimes an intra-squad game, other times against another organization who ran their league in Florida as well.

That fall, I was welcomed into the "Minnesota Twins Men of Steal." You had to have stolen at least twenty bases or more in a season. With my twenty-one, I barely made it; but considering that the rookie leagues played only half as many games as the A, AA, and AAA players, I did pretty well. Only five players in the organization had the required twenty stolen bases that year. The player named the "Minnesota Man of Steal," who had the most, had forty-two. Impressive, yes—but if I had played in the same number of games that he had and kept up my pace, I would have had forty-nine and led the entire organization. Not bad for a rookie.

I got back to Bensonhurst the first day of November, three days before my twenty-second birthday. Joe was back as well, and we were treated like rock stars. We had our own baseball cards! There I was on the front in my Twins uniform, bat in hand, focused on the ball leaving the pitcher's hand, with my stats printed on the back. Our pictures were hung in the neighborhood gym and in the pizzeria on my corner. We always made sure we had our cards with us—they were like free tickets into clubs and the VIP treatment, where we were asked to sign autographs.

We got invited to speak to young kids in the schools, where we were asked things like, "Do you make a million dollars?" and "How do you like playing against each other?"

But my favorite question was, "Who is your hero?"

I immediately answered then with the same answer that I give to this day.

My mom.

She will always be my hero. She taught me by example to work hard, to be strong, to be resilient, to never settle for second best, and to never expect anything to be handed to you. If you want it, you have to work for it, you have to earn it.

Joe and I worked out together throughout that winter. It's not easy to keep up your baseball skills when it's twenty degrees outside and as much as a foot of snow on the ground. We weren't in Florida anymore. For Joe, it was especially hard. His pitching arm was in constant pain. No matter what he did, short of surgery, it just wouldn't get better.

Finally, March arrived, and we were off to spring training. The season wasn't what either of us had hoped for. Joe finally had to tell the Reds about his arm pain, and he was released.

Terry Ryan, the Twins general manager, asked me after practice one day, "Why won't you run for me?"

I didn't know what to say. I had been voted the fastest player selected in the draft by the Twins just the year before. Had I worked too hard over the winter, making my legs heavy? Spring training ended, and I got my assignment—I was headed to Indiana to play in the Midwest League for the Fort Wayne Wizards.

Major league baseball teams, in addition to their big-league club, have six levels in their minor league organizations—two rookie teams, two A ball teams, one AA team, and a AAA team. I was hoping to at least make the higher A team, which played in Fort Myers. Instead, I was off to Fort Wayne, just one level up from my rookie year.

When I arrived, I was pleasantly surprised. The Wizards were only in their second year as the Twins lower A club. They had built a beautiful new stadium to attract the Twins. It seated 6,500 fans, with luxury boxes, a beautiful clubhouse with wooden lockers, and games televised on a local cable channel.

Chad had gotten married, so that season my roommates were Ben Jones, now an MLB scout, and Tommy Knauss, the fellow I played the card game with the year before. A month into the season, we made room for Torii Hunter, a first-round pick, after he was called up from extended spring training. I had a front row seat at second base to watch him rob batters of hits every day with his acrobatic catches in center field. Torii went on to play nineteen seasons in the bigs, was a five-time All-Star, and won nine Gold Gloves. Not only was he an incredibly gifted ball player, Torii is a warm and gentle soul. His faith in Jesus is rock solid—it was evident then, and even more so now.

A TV crew greeted us when we arrived, and photographers from the local paper snapped pictures that ran in the next issue.

They even printed the lineup for our first game—I knew I would be playing second base, but that's how I found out I was batting second and not leadoff.

That first game was an omen of what was to come that season. I went 0 for 5. It was really difficult, but I made a conscious effort not to allow my performance in any one game to affect my attitude.

I'm sad to say it, but I had more hitless games my second year in pro ball than good ones. While the year before I had multiple hitting streaks of ten games, eleven games, even one twenty-game stretch, that didn't happen playing for the Wizards. Instead, I had 0 for 20 slumps.

There was one major highlight for me during my time in Fort Wayne. The Twins big league team came into town to play us in an exhibition game. Our manager, Jim Dwyer, eighteen years in the big leagues himself, put me at leadoff for the game; and on the third pitch in the first inning, I hit an inside fastball down the left field line past the third baseman. I dove head-first into second for a double, and seven thousand people stood and cheered me on. Chuck Knoblauch, the Twins' big league second baseman, gave me a fist bump.

"Nice shot, Danny."

I felt like I had arrived, like a big leaguer in that moment. I went on to score the first run of the game. We had the lead. At least for a while.

Later in the game, we were in the field. Knoblauch was on first, and Kirby Puckett, one of the greatest players to ever put on a Twins uniform, hit a shot right at me. It took a wicked in-between hop, but I stayed in front of it. First it hit me on my wrist, then ricocheted off my chest. I stayed under control, picked up the ball and tossed it to my shortstop, just in time to force Knoblauch at second for the third out of the inning. He laughed and spoke to me again.

"Hey, that's a hit in the big leagues."

Kirby also smiled at me as I ran past him to the dugout.

"Hey, #23, that was highway robbery!"

I was up second in our half of that inning, warming up in the on-deck circle. The Twins' batboy came over.

"Mr. Puckett wants to know if you want him to sign that ball print on your arm."

I looked over to their dugout, and Kirby, one of my heroes, Dave Winfield, and several of the other Twins were looking at me and laughing. They had seen me looking at the mark the ball had left on my wrist. It has faded over the years, but if you look hard enough you can still see three stitch marks from that baseball. I took a shot, but I didn't let it knock me down.

If only the rest of that season had been so good. Baseball is such a head game. As one coach told me, the biggest difference between those who make it to the bigs and those who don't is what happens from the neck up. You don't get drafted as a professional baseball player if you don't have the skill set to play in the major leagues. It's how you deal with adversity, with the bad times, whether you let them get in your head or not that makes the difference between getting called up or getting cut.

I was making contact at the plate, but rather than balls getting through the infield like the year before, everything I hit seemed to be straight at someone. I lost my confidence. My playing time got cut when the Twins drafted a second baseman in the fourth round and sent him to our club.

What got me through that time was Baseball Chapel. It's a great thing they do in minor league baseball. Every Sunday morning there was a short, ten to fifteen-minute chapel program offered. Tom Hopewell (what a great name!) led our chapel services in Fort Wayne. He was a kind, gentle man who would stay behind after the service, talk with me, and answer any questions I had. I started reading my Bible, trying to keep my focus and stay positive.

I met with the Twins' psychologist and started reading sports psychology books. I practiced relaxation and concentration techniques. I arrived early at the stadium, before practice and before games, to spend extra time in the batting cage. My passion for the game I loved was as strong as ever, but it just wasn't reflected in my performance. I began to realize that there was a possibility that I might get cut. But I wasn't going to let it happen because I gave up, because I didn't put in the necessary work and effort to try and improve my play.

The low point came for me in Burlington, Iowa. For the first time in my baseball career, I was put at third base. Since junior high, I had always played shortstop or second base. Up the middle, it was all about speed and agility, two of my greater strengths. At third, it's about being alert and maintaining your concentration.

The Burlington field was known as the worst kept infield in the Midwest League. But my troubles that day weren't because of the field. Most of it was in my head. I lost all of my concentration and focus.

In the bottom of the second, I took a shot off of my kneecap. After that, I moved in, and the next ball skipped off the grass and went right past me. It was like the guys on the other team knew I was unfamiliar with that position. After that, I backed up on a ball, something I knew not to ever do, and I made another error. The official scorer gave me three errors in that one inning—which was generous on his part. He could have given me a couple more. Because of my play, the other team scored five runs. I'm sure our pitcher was cursing me under his breath. The Burlington fans piled on.

"Hit it to the third baseman. He can't catch a cold."

Cold indeed.

It was the first time in my baseball career that I wanted to walk off the field and give up. I had never experienced that awful feeling of knowing that my team lost because of the way I played, because of my errors. I wanted to disappear under a rock.

Somehow, and it had to be God's grace, I survived the 1994 season without getting cut. After having such a great rookie season, my average fell from .310 to .202 that year. I spoke with my scout, Herb Stein, and he told me that in his forty years in baseball, he had never seen a player's average drop by one hundred points. No doubt Herb meant well, because he always believed in me and felt like I was big league material, but I didn't find much comfort in those words.

After five months, I left Indiana and headed back to Brooklyn with a much different mindset than I had the year before. That previous winter, I had tried to remain humble and not brag about my performance, but I must admit that I had some pride when folks asked me about my play after that rookie season. This off-season, I wouldn't be so quick to blurt out my Wizards statistics.

I wrote .202 on a big card and put it right next to all of the awards I had received in baseball, hoping that would motivate me to get back to the way I knew I could play.

I tried to focus on what I had done well that season. Double plays were almost automatic. My arm was stronger, and I was throwing the ball harder than ever. Somehow, I remained confident that I would not get cut during that off-season, and the next year I would get back to hitting the way I did in 1993.

Twenty-six years later, I would need that kind of belief in myself to get up out of a hospital bed and back to my family.

CHAPTER FIVE

HEAD-ON

L ife was baseball and baseball was life—at least as far as I was concerned at that point in my life. I dreamed it, breathed it, envisioned it, and I worked really hard at it. I determined that I was going to do everything within my power to show the Twins that my rookie season was no fluke—the only fluke in my baseball career was going to be that one season in Fort Wayne.

I understood that I might be on the chopping block. The pittance I had been given to sign my contract was a drop in the bucket. If I wanted to survive the next season, I knew without a doubt I had to perform.

Unlike the day I waited with anticipation for the phone call to tell me I had been drafted, that fall I dreaded hearing the phone ring.

What if they're calling to cut me?

Before, I was excited to see a piece of mail with my name and the Twins logo on it. It meant finding out when to show up for spring training or where I might be playing that year. But that fall, I feared getting the letter that would tell me not to come back, that I had been let go. Using the

US Postal Service is a cold way to crush someone's dreams—but one commonly used by professional baseball organizations.

I distinctly remember how my prayer life picked up after that season. When things are going well for us, too often we forget God. We don't have a *perceived* need for him in our lives. But after the awful season I had, I certainly felt the need. I read my Bible, and I talked to God about my desire to prove that I was major league baseball material.

I moved back into my old neighborhood and lived with my mom. It was a little difficult for me, being a young adult now, and with four years away at college and two years of baseball travel behind me. But Mom was gracious, and loving, and encouraging. My siblings joined her in surrounding me with unconditional love and encouragement for my future.

As I began that off-season, the only real pressure I experienced was self-inflicted. My talent for the game never changed—my body could still perform at the highest level. The problem was above my shoulders, in my head. I read books on concentration, on relaxation. I tried to draw from what I had learned as a psychology major in college. What I later realized, as I grew and matured, is that there is a significant difference between reading something in a textbook, or even working with someone else and their problems, and actually applying what you have learned to your own life.

My friend, Joe, who had been released by the Reds back in the spring, was in the throes of adjusting to life without baseball. Working as a bank teller, he was going through a rough time. His dream had been taken away from him. We talked openly about it. He was always fully supportive of me, telling me that now I had to carry both of our dreams. My job was to make it to the Show and give him tickets to Twins games.

We worked out together like we had back in our school days. We played catch. I wasn't sure which was greater for Joe—the pain he still felt in his arm or the pain from being cut by the Reds.

About three weeks into being back home, Joe and I were out late the night of September 23, 1994. Earlier that evening we had been hanging out with our good friend, Sal. After I'm not sure how many drinks, we made the dumb decision to drive over to a club and meet a few friends. Sal drove his own car.

Joe and I were in his small Toyota Camry. In Brooklyn on Ridge Boulevard heading toward 78th Street, on our way to the club, I had one of my guardian angel moments. We were about seven blocks from the club at this point, but something told me to buckle my seat belt. I had ignored that little voice hundreds of times before. But this time, I didn't. I now know that decision saved my life. The last thing I remembered was looking down at the seat to find the latch beside me.

We were two stupid young men in our twenties acting like kids. Joe never should have gotten behind the wheel that night in his condition, and I never should have let him—or gotten in the car with him. We hit another car head-on, which caused our car to knock out a fire hydrant and the brick wall of a house at the corner of 78th and Ridge. You can still see, by the difference in the brick, where they repaired the front wall of that house. Eyewitnesses said that the car flipped over several times before coming to a stop.

Hey, kids, some words of advice here:

Don't drink and drive.
Don't let your friends drink and drive.
Don't get in the car with someone who has been drinking.

As far as I know, and thanks be to God, the two people in the other car were able to walk away from the accident. I never heard that they suffered any injuries.

Joe and I weren't quite that lucky.

Sal told us later that when we didn't show up at the club, he got back in his car and backtracked to find us. By the time he got to the scene of the accident, we had been taken away. Looking at the condition of Joe's car, Sal assumed it was to the morgue.

Joe and I were both knocked out by the initial impact with the other car. I'm not sure how long I was out, but when I came to, I was struggling to breathe. It wasn't too dissimilar from what I experienced lying in the hospital with COVID-19 twenty-six years later.

In that moment of panic, of feeling like I was about to take my final breath and die, my life flashed before me. But unlike the experience that others have described, it wasn't my *past* that I saw; I saw into my future. Three images, two moving and one still-life, swept across my mind. In the first moving image, I was standing at the front of a church, looking down the aisle toward the back. A woman with blonde hair stood there in a wedding dress, her father beside her.

The second moving image was of two young boys, slightly different in age, one bigger, one blonder, both smiling, having the time of their lives.

The third image, a still-life, was of an empty baseball field. It wasn't Yankee Stadium, which I know so well, and it wasn't the Metro Dome in Minnesota, where I hoped to play one day. I'm still not exactly sure what I was being shown with that image—perhaps my future role as a baseball coach, or maybe it's still to be revealed.

I'm not sure how long these images lasted. One second? Ten seconds? It felt like an eternity. But at that point, I came out of it and had some awareness of my surroundings.

The car was on its side, with my side down on the cement sidewalk. I knew I was dying, and in desperation I kicked out the windshield. Air rushed in, and I was able to breathe. Joe was still out cold and had fallen over on top of me. Using my left arm, I pushed him off and out the windshield opening. People had gathered around by this time and helped pull him out.

From the time I woke up, I prayed. I began with:

Please, God, let me live!

Once I was able to breathe after kicking out the windshield, it was:

Please, God, don't let me be paralyzed!

In my state of shock, I guess it didn't register that I must not be paralyzed, if I could push Joe off me and kick out the windshield. I remember being afraid to move, that perhaps I had a spinal injury that could be damaged further if I didn't remain still.

Then I felt the pain in my right arm. It was at that point that I understood why I only used my left arm to push Joe off me—my right arm was pinned between the car and the sidewalk.

As I became more and more aware of what had happened, my prayer changed again:

Please, God, don't let my arm be amputated.

I began to wonder whether or not I would ever be able to throw a baseball again.

The pain in my arm became unbearable. I was screaming in agony. The people who gathered were trying to do whatever they could to help. When they realized that my arm was caught under the car, they lifted the car enough for me to get my arm out. Once my arm was freed, I was afraid to look at it, worried that my baseball career was over.

I was stuck. They couldn't get either door open to pull me out.

Soon, the first responders arrived with the jaws of life and the ambulances to take us both away. Much of what happened then was a blur, probably because of the shock. Once they got me out of the car, they loaded me onto a spine board and took me to Kings County Hospital, the best trauma center in Brooklyn. As the ambulance pulled away with me in it, I remember looking at the gaping hole in Joe's mangled car where the roof had been.

Even with the pain and the disorienting shock I was experiencing, somehow I felt safe. My prayers helped me focus on God and kept me from feeling sorry for myself. The EMTs were professional, calm, and put me at ease. We arrived at the emergency room, where I spent the next six hours. They stuck tubes into just about every place they could in my body, even cutting a hole just below my navel for a tube to check for internal bleeding. While the insertion of the catheter was the most painful one going in, the one up my nose and down into my stomach was the most uncomfortable. Every time I tried to swallow, it felt like it was cutting into the back of my throat.

At one point, the whole team that was working on me suddenly disappeared. One minute someone was sewing up my face, someone else was sewing up my eye, and then they were gone. With a needle and thread hanging off the side of my face, dangling in my line of sight, I saw a passing nurse and asked her what was going on. She told me that someone had come in with a double barrel shotgun wound, and the trauma team had to rush to that person. I know it sounds terrible, but I was relieved when I heard that. I figured I was in much better shape than the guy they went to help.

When they finally got back to me, a medical student kept screwing up, trying to close a laceration in my head with a staple gun. The head emergency room doctor removed those staples, took the gun and blasted eight staples (I counted them) into my head in a matter of seconds. Nurses looked for glass in my hair and all over my body. I was helpless lying there. All I could do was pray.

They wheeled me away to take x-rays of my arms, my shoulders, and my back. I had a herniated disc at my L4/L5 vertebrae, which they discovered later in an MRI—an injury that still gets aggravated from time to time. While lying there, I felt something cutting into the back of my head. I told the x-ray technician that the nurses must have missed a piece of glass. He felt around in my hair and pulled an object out.

He looked at it in the palm of his hand with a look of surprise on his face, then a big smile.

"Jesus," he said, in a Spanish accent.

When he handed it to me, I believe we both had a Holy Spirit moment. I felt goose bumps, and I could tell that the technician did as well.

Although they took my chains off when I first arrived, Jesus had decided to stick around!

It was the head of Christ—a gold charm that had come off one of my chains. I still wear that charm to this day.

I was glad to have the pain in the back of my head stop, but even more thankful for the message God was sending me with that charm. I knew that Jesus was telling me:

Don't you worry, Dan. I've got this! I'm with you all the way.

I took that Christ head and held onto it the entire time I was in the hospital. They wanted to take it and put it with my chains and other personal items, but I refused to give it to them. Just like He told me that He was there with me, I wanted God to know that I was holding onto Him, and I needed Him to get me through this terrible time.

At some point, Mom and all my siblings showed up at the hospital. I still hadn't seen myself in a mirror, but I could tell from their faces that it must be pretty bad. With those tubes coming out of me everywhere, my face all swollen, and a piece of it hanging off to the side (which later required plastic surgery), I'm sure I was a mess to look at.

And yet, I knew that I had experienced a miracle. I have no doubt that God sent an angel to tell me to buckle my seat belt just before the accident. One of the doctors told me that I would be dead if I hadn't put it on—in emergency rooms, the passenger's seat is known as the death seat. Despite all the cuts and bruises and lacerations, I had no broken bones—even in my right arm. All the tests for internal bleeding or any other complications came back negative. Forty-eight hours after arriving at the hospital, I was released to go home.

God protected Joe just like he did me. Taken to a different hospital with lacerations on his head, he had no broken bones and was released a few hours after getting sewn up. God used me as a pretty good cushion to soften his fall!

While my hospital stay was short, my full recovery took a bit longer. For the next three months, I went to physical therapy three times a week. I started by lifting five-pound weights. I approached my healing from those injuries like I did my performing at an elite level on the baseball field. Before the accident, my goal was to be in better shape that off-season than I had been the season before. Now, before I could get any better, I had to get back to where I had been.

Day by day, one exercise at a time, pushing myself just a little bit harder so that I could see some improvement—that's how I did it. In all my time playing baseball, I had never been injured before, at least nothing beyond a scrape or a bruise. But here I was, first fighting for my life, and then fighting to keep my roster spot in the Twins organization.

From the first day in the hospital, I was determined to keep the Twins from finding out about the accident. I didn't want them to have one more excuse for releasing me. I thought I might get away with it, until the phone rang several days after the wreck.

"Hello, Dan. This is Jim Rantz with the Minnesota Twins."

"Oh, shit," slipped out under my breath.

He was the director of the Twins' minor league system. A huge lump came up in my throat and a knot in my stomach.

"Yes, sir. What can I do for you?"

"I heard you were in an accident. How are you?"

I lied. I'm not proud of that. But I did. I told him that yeah, I had been in a crash, but it was just a little fender-bender. No big deal. I was fine. Everybody was fine. Nothing to worry about. And I assured him that it would have absolutely no impact on my ability to play for the Twins in the spring. I told him how I was working out every day, getting stronger, and that I would be a better player in '95 than I had been in '94. I thanked him for reaching out, and we ended the conversation.

I don't know how he found out. Was there something in the papers that someone in the Twins organization read? Did one of my teammates hear and tell one person, who told someone else, until it eventually got back to him? Thinking about it now, it's possible that he knew all the details the whole time and simply went along with my lie during that phone conversation. Maybe he didn't want to embarrass a twenty-three-year-old kid who couldn't let go of his dream to make it to the big leagues.

Other than the lie about the accident, all that I told him proved true. During those months of rehab, I focused most of my attention on getting my injured arm back into shape. On January 3rd, I was out throwing the ball in the schoolyard like I did when I was a kid. Two weeks later, I left for the warm weather in Florida so that I could concentrate on reporting for spring training in March. My brother James lived in Fort Lauderdale at the time. I stayed with him while I trained and whipped my body into the best shape I had ever been in.

One more thing happened during that rehab period that I have never forgotten and that continues to impact the way I live my life.

Within days of being home from the hospital, God sent another of his guardian angels to speak to me. A former police detective, African American, older, overweight, and out of shape came huffing and puffing up the stairs to our apartment, sweat pouring off him, to speak with me about the accident. He had retired from the force and was working as an investigator. He needed to ask me some questions.

I don't remember anything about what he asked. And I don't remember what led him into what follows. I vaguely remember that we chatted for a while about life in general. But what I do distinctly remember is this exchange that took place at my Mom's dining room table.

He took a piece of paper and drew a Venn diagram—two circles beside each other, with a very slight overlap between them. First, he pointed to one of the circles.

"This is you," he said. "See all this space that isn't connected to the other circle? That's all the time you spend focused on yourself. You sleep, you go to work, you have all these things that will be in your life that have little or nothing to do with your wife. See this one?"

He pointed to the other circle. I nodded, wondering where this was going and if he realized that I wasn't married.

"That's your wife. She has a lot of the same stuff going on in her life, separate from you. Now see this?"

He took a pen and colored in the section where the two circles joined.

"This is the little bit of time in both of your lives that you have to invest in each other."

He put down the pen and looked me in the eye.

"Dan, I'm telling you, there's only a small window in life to spend with the one you love. Invest in that small time and make the most of it!"

As simple as that illustration is, it had a profound impact on me in that moment. And it has stayed with me through the years. Soon I'll tell you about meeting the woman God has blessed me with, and how He has given me the opportunity to fulfill that lesson.

CHAPTER SIX

ONE DREAM ENDS

My brother James had been in Florida for four years, working at a club in Fort Lauderdale. He welcomed me to come down to the Sunshine State and stay with him for about six weeks before spring training began, where I could be outside and really focus on getting myself into playing shape.

Once I traveled over to Fort Myers, I felt like I was in the best condition I had ever been in. I walked into the clubhouse that first day of spring training, and the only thing my teammates wanted to talk about was the big scar on my face.

I told them I cut myself shaving.

The news about my accident had gotten around, but I refused to talk about it. I was still afraid the Twins would use it as an excuse to release me, that I would be seen as a liability. There, in my locker, was a gray jersey. I was disappointed. It meant that I might be sent to Fort Wayne for another season. That gray jersey gave me even more motivation to prove to the Twins that I was ready to move up in the organization. Chad, my former roommate and still my batting cage partner every day before practice, had a blue jersey. He and a number of the other guys we had played with in Indiana were moving up to the Fort Myers club. I was determined to join them.

My good friend, Rob DeBrino, a relief pitcher from New Jersey who had played with us in Fort Wayne the year before, had a gray jersey as well. We had become close in Fort Wayne, and Rob had driven me back to Brooklyn after that awful season. Both of us are of Italian descent, both of us are from the tri-state area—we had a lot in common and remain close friends today. Our gray jerseys meant that we were working out that spring with the Fort Wayne club—our assignment was with a bunch of players who had played rookie ball in Elizabethton the year before.

I went on to have a really strong spring training. My defense was excellent, my arm strength was back and better than ever, and I raised my batting average to .350, hitting the ball on the nose almost every at bat. Rob was like Chad and me—he had the same work ethic. Never a showboat, he showed up ready to work hard and contribute to the team's success in any way the coaches needed. He had a wicked knuckle-curve that he could throw at any place in the count. We both had something to prove.

The big-league staff ran all of our practices that spring. It meant that I got to work with Tom Kelly, who was the manager of the Twins, which was a great experience. I think it really helped my game, but that spring was unusual—it was the year of a strike by the big-league players. Rather than having the Twins' normal roster around, we had replacement players in the clubhouse. These were mainly guys who had been out of baseball for a while and were looking for another shot at the big time. They were willing to cross the picket lines, unlike most of us in the minor league system.

I spent some time talking with one of those players, whose locker was right by mine. He had made it to the big leagues at one point in his career, if only for a few days. He told me that in his first game in the bigs, he faced Nolan Ryan, a pitcher ranked among the one hundred best players in baseball history. He went 1 for 2 that day with an RBI double. What an incredible memory and experience to have! Injuries, politics, and trades landed that guy back down in the minors until he was released. He talked with me about what it felt like to be out of the game we loved and how excited he was to have a second bite of the apple.

Spring training ended, and when final assignments were handed out to begin the season, Rob and I had blue jerseys hanging in our lockers. It might as well have been Christmas morning! It felt great to be rewarded for our hard work.

I was officially a member of the Fort Myers Miracle. What an appropriate name! It was a miracle that I was alive and able to play the game I loved at a high level. And I would be doing it with two guys who were great friends. Chad, Rob, and I encouraged one another, pushed one another, and probably competed with one another as to who worked the hardest. The season was off to a great start it seemed. My dream was coming true.

Our first two games were out of town against the Port Charlotte Rangers, and I didn't start at second base. But once we got back home to Lee County Stadium, my name was in the lineup. First time up, I hit a sharp grounder that got through the infield between the first and second basemen. It was like what happened my rookie year in Elizabethton—the balls that had left my bat and gone straight at an infielder in Fort Wayne were once again finding holes and getting to the outfield. I went 3 for 4 that game, with a triple down the right field line and a bunt past the pitcher that I ran out for a hit. My only out was a sharp line drive to the second baseman. The Miracle won, and I felt like I was winning my battle as a professional baseball player too.

I didn't start every game, but when I did, I played well. My confidence was back to where it had been my rookie year, and I was stronger and faster than ever. In one game against the Yankees, I had three infield base hits, which is very unusual for a right-handed hitter (left-handed batters have an advantage running out hits to first base, because their batting box is a couple of feet closer to that bag). My teammates said it looked like I was flying down the first base line.

Like many teams, the Miracle had a mascot—a golden retriever they called Jericho, the Miracle Dog. When Jericho passed away, the team honored him in a ceremony before a game with the Cardinals by sprinkling the dog's ashes on the edge of the infield, right where I played at second base. During the game, I had to dive for a ball up the middle. I came up with it, along with a mouth full of dirt. I threw the runner out, but when I looked over into our dugout, the guys were doubled over laughing. They thought I had swallowed poor Jericho.

Early in May, we had an away game in West Palm Beach against the Expos. In the top of the ninth inning, I drove in the game-winning hit, a line drive up the middle. In the bottom of ninth, with one out and runners on first and second, I made a diving catch on a ground ball up the middle. I threw the batter out at first. The runners advanced, but we were still up a run. Then, with runners on second and third and two outs, the next batter hit a line drive to my left. I made a diving stab to end the game and seal the win.

We were headed back home when our bus broke down in Florida's Alligator Alley. It's no place to be after dark. Fortunately, another bus was able to pick us up. The driver had dropped off a group of college cheerleaders at a camp and was heading back our way. Those of us who were single wondered what that trip might have been like if they had still been on that bus.

I was performing well, getting along great with my teammates, and playing the game I loved. What could possibly go wrong?

The next day I arrived at the field at 3 p.m. like I did every day before a 4:10 practice. Chad was already in the batting cage, hitting with Tommy Knauss. I put on my uniform and headed out to join them. I felt good, my mechanics were right, and my swing was in the groove—the ball was exploding off my bat. I had every hope that I would be in the lineup that night against the Rangers. With sweat dripping off me, I took another swing, and then I heard our first base coach, José, come back out to the cage.

"Hey, Danny. Al [Al Newman, our manager] wants to see you."

I thought that maybe he would say I was playing third that night (which occasionally happened), or that he wanted to go over some videotape of my play (that happened from time to time too). As I walked into the clubhouse, I saw Al walking toward me.

"What's up?" I asked.

He looked at me, stopped, and then said, "Forget it, Danny. Go on back out and hit."

I felt relieved.

It must not be anything too serious.

I rejoined Chad and Tommy in the batting cage. Ten minutes or so later, out comes José again.

"Hey, Danny. Al wants to see you now."

"I just got back from going in there. He said to forget about it."

"That was then. This is now. He says for you to come on in."

I walked through the clubhouse. Al wasn't in there, so I went down the corridor to his office. I had an eerie feeling that something wasn't right. The door was closed, so I knocked.

"Come in," he said. I didn't like the tone of his voice.

His hands were over his head with his face down on the desk.

"Shut the door."

I did, and he looked up.

"Danny, I don't know how to tell you this. But I have to let you go."

I couldn't believe what I'd just heard. It took a moment for it to sink in. And when it did, I was devastated. My batting average was on its way up, my defense was at its best, and I was the fastest guy on the team. Speechless, I fought to keep back the tears. Feeling abandoned, and somewhat betrayed, that moment was the worst feeling I'd ever had in my life.

"Danny, I know you can play at a higher level," Al continued with his eyes full of water. "But there's nothing I can do. It's out of my hands. I tell you, this is the hardest thing I've ever had to do as a coach."

Finally, I got my voice.

"Come on, Al. You know I'm hitting the ball well. My numbers are improving every day. Just last night I not only got the game-winning RBI, but I made two great plays at second to end the game! Is there any hope of changing your mind?"

"If it was up to me, Danny, of course I would. But this comes from higher up. I just called the head of our farm system.

That's why I sent you back out to hit some more. I tried, Danny. I tried to get him to keep you. But the decision has already been made. I'm sorry."

This was the same guy who had called me within a few days of my accident.

I stood there, frozen in disbelief that my dream was ending in an office. Al went on.

"You're the hardest worker on this team. You and I both know that. Sometimes this game just isn't fair."

"So, can I at least play tonight? Just one more game?"

I don't know how I thought I would be able to play in the condition I was in, but I was ready to try anything to pretend this was all a nightmare, one that I could still wake up from.

"No, Danny, they've already sent someone else down. He's filling your roster spot."

Al Newman had been a utility player, a hustler, primarily a second baseman who played on two World Championship teams. He had the rings to prove it, one in 1987 and the other in 1991, with a career average of only .220. He understood what it meant to pour your heart and soul into a game that you loved, a game that you had to work at harder than everyone else to prove that you deserved your shot. Even through my pain, I could tell that he saw a bit of himself in me.

There was nothing else left to say. In a daze, I walked out of his office. It hit me then that the hardest part was still to come. How could I face my teammates? How could I go back into the clubhouse, pack my stuff, and leave without anyone else finding out? My hands trembled. My legs were shaking. I was losing the battle to keep the tears from falling.

I stopped by the bathroom and threw cold water on my face before I went into the clubhouse. I determined to go straight to my locker, throw my stuff quickly into a bag, and try to get out of there before anyone noticed. Rob was sitting by my locker. At first he didn't notice anything, then he saw me rubbing my eyes. I couldn't speak—I gave him the "cut" sign by running my finger across my throat. I could tell he was shocked. When one of our teammates started walking by, I put my finger up to my lips to tell him not to say anything.

I left without saying a word and without anyone saying anything to me. I walked out through the darkened tunnel underneath the stadium that led into the parking lot. Usually there's hope for a light at the end of a tunnel. But even with the bright Florida sunshine beaming down that May afternoon, I couldn't see any light at the end of the tunnel I faced.

I heard the crack of the bat coming from the batting cages. The sound that I loved now sounded like gunshots, causing me to flinch. That's when I totally lost it. The tears poured. A decision had been made that changed my whole life, a decision that I had no control over. They weren't even sending me down to Fort Wayne. It was over. The dream had ended.

Rob must have told Chad, who came out and caught me in the parking lot.

"What the [bleep] happened?"

He was furious.

I handed him two of my bats. They weren't going to do me any good anymore.

I found out later that he went on quite a hitting streak using those bats.

My college buddy, Butch Burrough, had been released by the Astros and was playing in a California independent league that year. He had flown out and had left his car with me to drive. I got behind the wheel of his Lincoln Continental, one of those huge, solid steel land yachts, put my head down, and bawled like a baby. I finally got it together enough to go back to our empty apartment after stopping to pick up a case of beer first.

When I walked in the door, the phone rang. It was Rob.

"Al called a team meeting right after you left. He told the whole team, 'I just had to let one of the hardest workers on this team go. It should have been one of the lazy dogs still sitting in this clubhouse instead of that great kid.' And he walked back to his office."

That should have made me feel better. Usually, when someone is released, the players talk about it for a minute among themselves, but there's never a team meeting about it. The team was shocked by the news. But even hearing about that speech didn't help me.

Turns out, the speech did help the team—I found out later that they went on a winning streak. Just like my bats helped Chad and his hitting, Al's speech motivated the rest of the players to hustle a bit more.

I stuck around Fort Myers for a few days, not sure what to do with myself. I called my brother James in Fort Lauderdale and told him what happened. He told me to drive down to stay with him until I could decide what to do.

Before I left Fort Myers, Rob gave me a handwritten note:

Dear Danny,

It really sucks to see you go. But you must go on with your life. You're the greatest person I have ever met, and you are a true friend. Life has other things in store for you. We might not know at this time, but the Lord has something else planned. Stay true to yourself, and don't let anyone or anything hurt the good person that I know. Please stay in touch with me and know that you are in my prayers. We have a lot of great memories between us that will hopefully put a smile on your face in this time of depression. Good luck, and I hope you get picked up by some other team. See you again soon, and always remember you have a friend in Rob DeBrino.

Your friend,
Robby D

Rob's letter really got through to me and made me feel better. As I read it, I knew that the Lord did have something else planned for me. A man of strong Christian faith, Rob's friendship has proven true again and again through the years.

I got to Fort Lauderdale to stay with James, in no hurry to rush home and look for a-nine-to-five job. For a few weeks, I would hang out at the beach in the morning, go to the gym in the afternoon, and hit the clubs at night. I was looking to have some fun and kill the pain. Several nights of the week I was at the place where James worked security, Club Mirage. Having James there with me was a God-send—he helped keep me from spiraling down into the abyss.

James decided to drive back with me to Brooklyn. We loaded all of our stuff in the car and headed home. It felt very strange to be there before summer had arrived. I refused to go into my favorite pizzeria on the corner or my favorite video store, places where they had my baseball card on the wall.

Mom didn't talk about my being released. I could tell that she was hurting because I was hurting. What she did do was give me, as she always had, her unconditional love and support. My sister, Janet, came over, and so did my older brother, John. Our close-knit family became even closer than we had before.

But with all that closeness, it started feeling a bit too close living with Mom in our small Brooklyn apartment. Janet told me that the basement apartment below her on Staten Island was coming available, so I moved into my own space. About the same time, Janet got me an interview with the securities firm she worked for on Wall Street.

It was my first interview for a real job. I felt nauseated, my tie was choking me, and the brand new, too-tight dress shoes felt nothing like my broken-in baseball cleats. Instead of standing at the plate in my uniform with a bat in my hand, I was sitting in front of a gentleman who didn't seem to get it. He wanted to know my work experience, my computer skills, with no appreciation for my work ethic, my self-discipline, my leadership skills, my understanding of and commitment to work with a team to meet a specific goal. I never settled for just doing what was asked of me—I always gave more. This guy failed to see the excellent employee he could have had in me.

I left there in emotional turmoil. One person's opinion had cost me my life-long dream—what I had worked for, prepared for, what I believed I was made for my entire life. I took some time to think about it, possibly obsessing over it. I knew I had the physical tools. Up to that point, I had taken the approach that if I outwork you, I can accomplish anything. Obviously, that had proven not to be enough. I decided that I needed to work on the mental aspect of my approach to baseball. My fitness was fine. If my game ever suffered, it was always because of my mental focus.

I began to try and figure out how to get back to professional baseball. I called my friend Neil, who introduced me to his agent in Los Angeles. He signed me over the phone. He sent out letters to every big-league organization, as well as the independent teams around the country. No big-league teams responded, but several of the independent teams did. I had two offers—one in Utah, an independent team that played in a league against the major league organizations' rookie teams, and the Mobile Baysharks in Mobile, Alabama. They played in the Texas Louisiana League, which was supposed to be one of the better independent leagues in the country.

I wasn't thrilled, but I wanted to play baseball much more than I wanted a nine-to-five job. I didn't want to go all the way back to playing like a rookie, so I hopped a plane to Mobile.

I was picked up at the airport along with Jack, a third baseman who had just been released by the Texas Rangers. We went to the field and practiced together, just the two of us, since the team was on the road in Corpus Christi, Texas. The next morning we were driven three hours to an airport in Mississippi, where we were to catch a plane to meet up with the team. But when we got to the airport, Jack handed his uniform back to the driver and said he was done. Baseball, once his love and passion, had instead become a source of pain and disappointment.

I began to see that when a dream dies, it takes a lot out of you. I left for Texas by myself, and Jack booked a flight for his home in Philadelphia.

When I arrived in Corpus Christi, I met the Baysharks' manager, Butch Hobson. A few years earlier, he was the skipper for the Boston Red Sox. I was excited to get to play for a big-league manager. Here was a guy who used to pencil Roger Clemens into his lineup card. Now he would be penciling in my name.

My first game as a Bayshark, I walked out into 102-degree heat. The suffocating air of Corpus Christi sucked the breath out of me. I felt like I had stumbled into an open oven. I went one for four that night with a stolen base. I don't know if it was the heat or the lingering disappointment of being cut by the Twins, but the joy of the game just wasn't there.

The next night, I hit the longest home run of my professional career. I hadn't hit very many in my three years. The center field fence was 420 feet away, and the ball cleared it easily. But as I rounded second on my home run trot, I knew it was time. I felt no thrill. Baseball was no longer life to me. There was no more passion, no more excitement, no love left for the game. I didn't want to be one of those guys who hangs on too long.

I went to the office and spoke with Butch.

"Coach, it's time. I'm hanging it up and going back home."

We talked for a bit. He thanked me for my honesty, showed me respect, and wished me well.

Just when I thought I was done for good, my college buddy, Butch Burrough, called once I got back home. His team in Long Beach, California needed a shortstop. The opportunity to be in sunny California with my great friend sounded too good to pass up.

A week later, I realized that I should have passed it up. Like the Righteous Brothers sang, that lovin' feelin' was gone, gone, gone, for the game I had loved all my life. I turned in my uniform for the last time.

Back home in New York, for the rest of that summer I was lost. I went back to the basement apartment on Staten Island below my sister. My older brother, John, helped me get a job with FedEx. I worked from 2 p.m. until 10 p.m. delivering packages. It was a great schedule for the partying lifestyle I chose: out at the clubs late at night, searching for my soulmate in all the wrong places, and then sleeping it off in the morning to start all over again in the afternoon.

The guys at the FedEx station wanted me to slow down. My baseball hustle had shifted to my delivery style, and I was making them look bad by delivering a lot more packages in an eight-hour shift than they were.

Meanwhile, my best friend, Joe, had gotten a position as a fitness trainer. He talked me into coming over and getting a job with him. I never thought that I would be doing that for the rest of my life, but God had a plan! At first what I loved about it was getting to work in shorts and a t-shirt—that was great.

But then I fell in love with working with people.

I was making a difference in the lives of others—a positive influence. I began to see the importance, and I began to learn how to apply the mental motivation and focus necessary to live a life of accomplishment. For me, working as a fitness trainer and later as a life coach was a better service than delivering packages. I went on to receive my certification as a trainer through the American College of Sports Medicine, a highly regarded organization in that field.

My dream of being a major league baseball player had come to an end. But I began to see that life had other dreams to offer.

CHAPTER SEVEN

ANOTHER DREAM BEGINS

While I was growing confident in my vocation as a fitness trainer, my search for a soulmate had hit a dead end. I went on dates—but with every one of them I knew right away that it wasn't going anywhere. No spark. No magic. No *This is the love of my life*. Frankly, I was starting to forget about it, or at least give up hope of finding that one special person.

Two years passed after my release by the Twins. That third summer, on July 13, 1997, I planned a trip down to Joey Harrison's Surf Club at Ortley Beach on the Jersey Shore. Up until this time in my life, I had never spent summers at the beach—baseball consumed those months. But during those years, the Surf Club became a favorite hangout for some of my friends and me. On that particular Sunday morning, I couldn't get anyone to drive with me, so I arranged to meet Joe and some other buddies at the Surf Club later that afternoon.

I left my apartment on Staten Island sometime between 9 and 10 a.m., and as soon as I hit the Garden State Parkway, I was in bumper-to-bumper traffic. Lanes and lanes of it. Ortley Beach is at Exit 82—by Exit 98, I was ready to change my plans and get out of that traffic.

I knew Point Pleasant Beach, which was off Exit 98, because I had been there several times with family and friends. It's nice, with a boardwalk, a pier, a tiki-bar, and Jenkinson's, a restaurant with outdoor seating overlooking the beach.

I parked, took my chair and blanket out to set up home base on the beach near the boardwalk, and went up to Jenkinson's for lunch. I got a great outdoor table where I could look out at the ocean. Older folks, couples and their kids, surfers with their boards, and girls in their bathing suits greeted my eyes. Because of my fitness training, I always try to eat healthy—so I ordered a salad with grilled chicken. Of course, I was at the beach, so a beer to wash it down seemed appropriate for the occasion.

Just after I placed my order, it happened. A beautiful young woman walked below me on the beach. She looked up at me and smiled. She immediately had my attention.

I tried to watch where she went, but I lost sight of her in the crowd once my food arrived. The whole time I was eating, I was combing the beach for her with my eyes. I wolfed the salad down, guzzled my beer, and headed back to my chair. I couldn't stop thinking about the girl with the blonde hair in the black one piece.

I had taken a book with me to read—*The Deep End of the Ocean* by Jacquelyn Mitchard. It was on the *New York Times* bestseller list and was marketed as a great summer beach book—*"a twist that will spin you around."* Just as I settled into my chair and pulled out the book, she walked past me again, smiled, and went to sit with a few other people nearby. She turned several times to smile at me. I was intrigued.

Between staring at a blank page in my book, which I was holding upside down, and trying not to be too obvious by staring at her, I kept looking over, trying to figure out her situation. She was with two girls, a guy, and a toddler. I definitely didn't want to approach her in that group setting. When none of the others were looking, I motioned for her to come over.

Before I knew it, she was by my side. We introduced ourselves. I found out her name was Heather. She wiggled her toes in the sand, and we talked like we had known each other all our lives. She was so comfortable to be with. Our conversation flowed easily for half an hour or so. She told me that she taught deaf, blind, and autistic children at a private school. I could tell that she was truly special—a heart of gold to go with her knock-me-out good looks.

We went up to Jenk's and continued our conversation over a beer. I certainly had forgotten about meeting my friends at Joey's on Ortley Beach! Far too soon she had to go—her family was getting ready to leave. I asked if I could have her number. She got a pen and piece of paper from the waitress and gave it to me.

I walked down to the beach with her and over to her family. She introduced me briefly to two of her sisters, Cheryl and Jennifer, her brother-in-law, Joe, and her one-year-old niece, Judi Mae. Watching her interact with her niece, I knew she would be a great parent. She said later she thought the same of me.

I couldn't stop thinking about Heather for the next few days. I agonized over when I should call—I didn't want to come across as desperate by calling too soon, and I didn't want her to think that I wasn't interested by waiting too long. On Tuesday, I picked up the phone and called. I asked her out for that coming Saturday night.

Heather lived in Little Falls, New Jersey, the working-class town where she taught, in a townhouse with two roommates. I took the Goethals Bridge from Staten Island to the New Jersey Turnpike for the hour drive to her place. I remember worrying about what to wear before I left my apartment—I wanted to make a good impression. I didn't want to be too casual, but I also didn't want to come across as a stiff by being overdressed. Khakis and a collared shirt seemed about right.

She answered the door, and I know my chin must have dropped to the sidewalk—she was stunning with her hair up, standing there in a brown dress with spaghetti straps. She looked like a movie star or runway model. We went into the city for dinner at South Street Seaport—about a forty-minute drive. I thought the restaurant overlooking the harbor would be a romantic spot. I had butterflies in my stomach and nerves like it was my first time up at the plate in the big leagues. Being with her, I knew I was.

We ordered the same thing—pasta with chicken and vegetables and a couple of glasses of wine. Like at the beach, talking with her was so easy. She was just as interested in learning about me as I was about her. We learned more about our families and the work we were doing at the time. After dinner, we walked out on the pier, and I held her in my arms for the first time.

There it was—the spark. And I felt it—the magic. I began to think that I had truly met my soulmate. We were like two puzzle pieces fitting perfectly together. We spent at least an hour on the pier, and we kissed. I felt electricity course through my entire body. In the moonlight, I could see goose bumps on her shoulders and arms, just like the ones I had.

"Are you feeling what I'm feeling?" I asked her.

She smiled. Words weren't necessary for her to tell me she was.

We sat and looked out at the Brooklyn Bridge suspended over the East River. The lights from the bridge and the Brooklyn Queens Expressway reflected off the water, which gently rippled below us. I took her hand in mine, and again we made a perfect fit.

My dream of being a big-league baseball player had ended. But I felt like my dream of finding a soulmate was coming true right in front of my eyes—eyes that fought back tears of joy, which I saw reflected in hers as well. I probably would have proposed to her right then and there if I thought it was socially acceptable. To know someone for less than a week, to have only spent three hours or so with her, and already believe that I wanted to marry her—was that possible?

When I took her home, we sat in the car and talked a bit longer in front of her apartment. Another kiss, and on my ride back to Staten Island all I could think about was this woman I knew I would marry. I'm convinced that we both knew that night.

Around that same time, I had a client in New York, one of the top doctors in the city, who was deeply in love with her husband. Before I met Heather, I remember us talking about finding that one special someone. I asked her:

"How do you know?"

"You'll just know," was all she could tell me.

I just knew.

We were together every weekend for the rest of that summer and well into the next school year. We went back to Point Pleasant Beach, to Atlantic City, and for long walks in Central Park. We jogged and worked out together, went on picnics, and went hiking at Harriman Mountain an hour north in New York state. We went to concerts—Hootie & the Blowfish, Stevie Nicks, and Frankie Valli and the Four Seasons where we sang "You're Just Too Good to Be True" to one another.

Within a month of meeting, we introduced each other to our families. I was twenty-five years old, and my mom had only met two of my previous girlfriends. Not just anyone got to meet Mom! My entire family immediately fell in love with Heather—her warmth, her sincerity, her internal beauty that shone through, lighting up every room she entered.

I soon learned that her mother had passed away after a battle with cancer a year before we met. Hers was a close-knit family. I watched the six girls interact with their dad, whom they loved and adored. Paul Englehardt, or Mr. E as I later called him, was quite intimidating to me at first. The mayor of Hawthorne, New Jersey, he was a very successful owner of several businesses due to his strong work ethic and impeccable character. I envied and respected how much this family enjoyed being together, and I longed to be the type of father whose children would feel the same about me. I wanted what that family had.

Nine months into our dating, I bought Heather an engagement ring. I knew I needed to have "the talk" with Mr. E before popping the question. Not long after purchasing the ring, we were at his house, and Heather was in the basement on the treadmill. I was extremely nervous, but I felt like this was my opportunity. Heather and I had planned a trip to Disney World the coming weekend, and I hoped to have our magic moment at the Magic Kingdom.

After he and I had a couple of beers, I decided to make my move. I asked if the two of us could go outside and take Louie, his schnauzer, for a walk. He gave me a look, and then we went out into their beautiful backyard—manicured landscaping surrounded the tennis court and swimming pool.

After a little more small talk, I decided to jump in with both feet.

"With your permission, I'd like to ask Heather to marry me. I promise you, I will treat her like gold."

The father of six daughters, with several already married, he didn't blink but continued walking as he spoke.

"They all say that."

Then he stopped and looked me in the eye.

"But the girls all say nice things about you."

And that was his answer.

A few days later, on April 14, 1998, Heather and I were at Epcot. The sun was setting over the water in the center of the international pavilions, and I had the ring in my pocket. I picked a spot on a bench in "Mexico," just outside the restaurant. We sat, and just before I got down on my knee, an older couple joined us and started talking. Not to be deterred, I took Heather into the restaurant for dinner, and before our meal arrived, I did it.

Ring out of my pocket, down on my knee:

"Heather Lee Englehardt, will you marry me?"

"What did my dad say?" were the first words out of her mouth.

"Come on, Heather!" I couldn't take the suspense. "Is that a yes?" I asked.

"Yes!" she said with a big smile.

She told me that Father Geno had to perform the ceremony.

Growing up, her family had been Protestant. Though they were not weekly church attenders, they prayed together at dinner, before bedtime, and had an affirmed faith in Jesus Christ. The year before we met, however, when Heather's mom passed away, not having a strong faith community to surround them left a weak wall in their spiritual sanctuary. Mr. E was lost for a time—losing his wife in her early fifties, left with six girls without a mother's influence. He drank much more than usual and floundered in his faith. Into that gap stepped a young priest, Father Geno Sylva, who served as God's messenger during this very trying time, the rector of St. Anthony's Parish in Hawthorne.

Because of Mr. E's position as mayor, Father Geno heard of his loss. He reached out.

How was he doing?

How was he dealing with his grief?

How were the girls dealing with their grief?

At the request of their father, he came over to talk with them about Heaven and the afterlife, and how to cope with the loss of a loved one. At one of those sessions with Father Geno, they went around the room trying to answer that unanswerable question:

Why? Why did their mother have to die so young?

When the time came for Heather to speak, she gave the only answer that made sense to her, speaking from the depths of her grief.

God must have needed an angel.

Father Geno affirmed the way she and the others were dealing with their loss. Two of her sisters invited Heather to join them for RCIA—Rite of Christian Initiation of Adults classes—but at first she was indifferent. They persisted. Finally, Heather agreed. Three of the six daughters, Heather included, converted to Catholicism.

For me, it shows God's hand in the perfect timing for the two of us to meet. There's a wonderful passage in the Bible, in St. Paul's letter to the Romans:

> *We know that all things work for good for those who love*
> *God, who are called according to his purpose*
> *(Romans 8:28).*

Not all things are good. I don't believe that death is a good thing—it's never God's perfect plan. Death is a leftover consequence of humanity's fall from God's grace. The Good News of Jesus Christ is that even the bad things, even death itself, can be turned into good in the loving hands of our good God.

Using Father Geno as his instrument, God took the pain of their family's loss and used it for good to bring them into His Church. And He used it for good by setting the stage for me to come into Heather's life, and her into mine, a year later. Her conversion to Catholicism made our marriage much easier on me, a lifelong Catholic. It meant we could be married in the Church with no problem. I was more than happy for Father Geno to marry us.

And so, there in the Mexican restaurant at Disney World's Epcot, Heather Englehardt agreed to marry Daniel Venezia. The magic happened, and we laughed, we cried, and we hugged. The rest of the restaurant roared its approval. That night was the best night I ever had in my life.

Father Geno moved from the local parish to serve as the President of DePaul High School, but he agreed to celebrate our wedding mass in St. Anthony's. We had several premarital counseling sessions with him, and I soon understood the family's love for this man. Charismatic, caring, and bearing a powerful anointing of the Holy Spirit, he was impressed that not only did I bring my Bible to our sessions, but I had actually read it!

God would send this man back into our lives at a later time, and he was there for me as one of my living guardian angels when COVID-19 struck.

Six months after our engagement, within fifteen months of our first meeting, we were married.

On October 2, 1998, the ceremony was held in St. Anthony's Church. Standing at the front of the church, looking back down the aisle, I realized that God had given me a vision of my wedding in that split-second moment I awoke from the head-on collision. This was the church in my vision, Heather was the bride dressed in white, and Mr. E was the father ready to bring her down the aisle so we could be joined in holy matrimony.

We had a large wedding party. Two of Heather's sisters were the maid and matron of honor, with her other sisters, my sister, and Heather's best friend making up the bridesmaids; while my two brothers served as co-best men and five of my closest friends acted as groomsmen. Father Geno was awesome during the ceremony, and the reception afterwards—at the Crystal Plaza in Livingston, New Jersey—was very special thanks to Heather's detailed planning and her father's generosity. A live band, great food, and wonderful family and friends created a joyous celebration for over two hundred guests.

The dream continued with our honeymoon in Europe—Paris, Venice, and Rome. In Paris, we stayed in a hotel right by the Louvre on the Left Bank. We toured Notre Dame and other beautiful churches, walking hand-in-hand for miles and miles in the romantic City of Love. Next, we took the world-famous Orient Express from Paris to Venice, the city my family is named after. During the train ride, we enjoyed a baguette and a bottle of wine as we watched historic scenery pass outside our window. The food, the culture, and the canals of Venice gave us memories to last a lifetime. We ended our honeymoon in Rome, where we visited the Vatican.

Our marriage could not have had a more charmed beginning.

Back home, we settled into a brand-new apartment in West Paterson, New Jersey, now called Woodland Park, that sat above a pizzeria and a couple of other stores. It was close to Heather's work at the school in Little Falls, close to her family, and I had the same commute into Manhattan that I had from Staten Island. We lived off what I made and put Heather's salary toward buying a house.

Back when I was with the Twins, Jim Lemon—a former major league player who came to fame when he finished third to Mickey Mantle and Roger Maris in their home run season of 1961—once told me, "The harder you work, the luckier you get."

I felt like I was the luckiest man alive. I'm sure you've heard the phrase:

When God closes a door, He opens a window.

For me, I now understood that the exact opposite had happened. God may have closed the window of opportunity for me to fulfill my dream of being a big-league baseball player, but by leading me to get off the Garden State Parkway at Exit 98 on the morning of July 13, 1997, he threw open the door of fulfillment and joy I experience every day with my soulmate, my best friend, my everything.

How could life possibly get any better than that?

CHAPTER EIGHT

FORGIVENESS

As I've said before, family is important to me. Our love of family was one of the things that attracted Heather and me to each other. A couple of my relatives, however, were distinguished by their absence at our wedding. I had made the decision, which I later regretted, not to invite my paternal grandmother to the ceremony and reception (my grandfather had passed away years before). I was afraid that my father would see the invitation and show up uninvited. All I could think about was my sister Janet's wedding, nine years earlier, with my mom and oldest brother walking her down the aisle, and our father taking up one of the front pews—so close to what was happening, but so distant and unwelcome in all of our relationships.

Perhaps that feeling of regret, of not inviting my grandmother to our wedding, played a part in what happened to me one night a little over a year into our marriage.

In addition to family, our faith also was an important part of our newly married life together. We attended services at the local parish church near our apartment in West Paterson. On this particular night, Heather had gone to bed early, while I remained sitting up in the living room of our apartment, reading my Bible and saying my prayers.

When I was a kid, I remember going to confession with my friends, and we would talk about our penance afterwards.

"How many did you get?"

"Twenty Our Fathers and thirty Hail Marys!"

That night, like many nights, I was on autopilot reciting the Lord's Prayer, like I had hundreds, probably thousands, of times in my life:

Our Father,
Who art in heaven;
Hallowed be thy name.
Thy kingdom come;
Thy will be done,
On earth as it is in heaven.
Give us this day our daily bread.
And forgive us our trespasses,
As we forgive those who trespass against us…

And I stopped.

Or better yet, something, or Someone, stopped me.

There wasn't an audible voice that I know of, but the thought hit me:

How can I be forgiven for my sins, if I haven't forgiven those who have sinned against me?

And the next thought horrified me:

What if none of my sins have been forgiven!

Inspired by the Holy Spirit, the writer of Hebrews in the New Testament wrote these words almost two thousand years ago:

> *Indeed, the word of God is living and effective, sharper than any two-edged sword, penetrating even between soul and spirit, joints from marrow; and able to discern reflections and thoughts from the heart (Hebrews 4:12).*

That's what Christ's words, in the prayer he taught us to pray, did to me in that moment. They cut through to reveal my need to forgive.

I started going through my list of those whom I still needed to forgive.

The girlfriend who cheated on me.

Check. I forgave her.

A friend who double-crossed me.

Check. He's forgiven.

The family member who still owed me money.

Check. Forgiven.

The guy who cut me off the night before. In the church parking lot!

All forgiven. Not too long a list. Nothing too heavy or weighty that I couldn't easily forgive. I got through those rather quickly and thought that perhaps my eternal soul wasn't in too much danger after all.

But then another person came crashing into my mind, into my soul.

My father.

The man I had seen maybe a dozen times from the age of twelve until that night. The man I tried to ignore if I ran into him at my grandparents' home, causing my grandmother to tell me, "Danny, show a little respect. At least say hello and goodbye to your father."

I remembered the time when I was three or four, and I was jumping on the bed. He slapped me across the side of my face. I cried, and I said to him, "You can't do that!"

Then he slapped me on the other side of my face.

I never jumped on the bed again.

I remembered hearing the story of the FBI coming and closing down two businesses he'd opened with embezzled money. My father had somehow gotten a job with one of New York's tugboat firms, working in the bookkeeping or accounting department. Out of nowhere, he quit that job and started two businesses—J's Unisex Shop and a small club with a bandstand in the corner, The Tugboat. My brother James remembers watching the FBI come in and take our father away before they shut down the club.

Somehow, he managed to never do any time for cooking the books at the tugboat company and embezzling that money.

I remembered a lot of other things he did to Mom, to my brothers, my sister, and me. He always tried to be the big man, wanting people to think he was something he wasn't. He wore a pinky ring and shiny suits with his shirt open at the chest. He would spend all of his money at bars buying drinks for everybody, trying to impress. He wanted people to think he was a tough guy. He was tough all right—hitting his kids and his wife. He was consistently inconsistent. He was unpredictable with his abuse, which was physical, emotional, verbal, mental, and spiritual.

I remembered my trip back to Brooklyn from Florida with James after I was cut by the Twins. Before going to Mom's, we stopped by our grandparents' house. I was talking with my grandfather about a speeding ticket I had gotten, about being cut and the end of my dream of being a big-league ball player, about what was next in my life.

My father was there, along with his brother, my Uncle Tom—who had been more of a father to me than he had. My father started talking to me like he was, well, my father. Like he had the right to speak about my life, to give me advice. I was in no mood to hear it. I got up to walk away, but I wanted to shut him up before I did.

"You're a cheat—and I'll never cheat on my wife. And as far as I'm concerned, any man who lays a hand on a woman is not a man."

I was twenty-three when I said those words. Perhaps with a little more maturity, I would have handled the situation differently. I know I would say something different today. My father's response?

"You'll see. You'll cheat. And every once in a while, a woman deserves a slap."

Really, God? This is the man you want me to forgive?

I thought about when I was still in college, and I visited my grandfather in the hospital. My father was there in the room. As I started to leave, he pulled a hundred dollar bill out of his wallet and handed it to me. I looked at it, looked at him, crumbled the bill and tossed it into the trash can as I walked out.

The last time I had seen my father flashed through my mind. My mom had retired from the bank, and her pension was about to kick in. Because she had never legally divorced my father, the concern was raised that he might try and go after her assets. For Mother's Day, soon after Heather and I were married, I gave Mom the gift of a divorce from my father.

The attorney who handled it said that the divorce papers could be delivered in one of two ways—I could pay for someone to deliver them, or I could deliver them myself. I had the money to pay someone the hundred bucks or so to do it. But I chose to do it myself.

At the time, yet again, he was staying at my grandmother's house. I walked in and handed him the papers. He immediately started yelling, screaming, cursing at me. I tried to remain calm. I walked over and gave my grandmother a kiss on the cheek.

"I love you, Grandma," I said as I was leaving.

"You don't love shit!" he screamed at me as I closed the door.

Those were the last words I had heard from my father.

And still God wanted me to forgive him—not for that alone, but for everything. For all the hurt, all the pain, all the anger, all the guilt, all the shame that he had caused the rest of my family and me.

Up to that point in my life, I believed that you didn't offer forgiveness to anyone who didn't ask for it. I had to think rationally, keep my guard up. *If there's a person in the room who has stolen from you, you don't leave your wallet out when you leave the room.*

I held onto unforgiveness against my father in a vain attempt to protect myself. Now God was asking me to let go.

I got down on my knees in the living room.

"God, you know this is hard. I'm gonna need your help. But if you are willing to forgive me—and I know you are!—I know that I need to be willing to forgive him."

And then I started saying these words over and over—

"Lord, please take the hate out of me. Lord, please take the hate out of me. Lord, *please* take the hate out of me…"

I fell asleep on the living room floor, repeating those words.

I don't know how long I was lying there, but when I woke up, the room was filled with luminous rays of bright, white light. They came from above me, from beside me, from beneath me. I could feel them penetrating every part of my being—spirit, mind, and body. I was filled to overflowing with what could only have been the Holy Spirit of the living God.

Immediately after I had that feeling of being filled, the floodgates opened and I was emptied. And then it all happened again.

It was like hitting the "refresh" button on a computer, over and over. I was filled, then emptied. Filled, then emptied. Filled, then emptied.

I felt clean. Absolved. It felt so good that I didn't want it to end. But it was also so powerful that I didn't know if I could take anymore—I couldn't wait for it to end.

It was the most exhilarating and the most exhausting feeling and experience I have ever had. I went into a full body cramp. If you've had a cramp in your leg, or your foot, just imagine your entire body cramping like that. Chills ran over me—but multiplied by twenty million compared to any chill I'd ever had before.

I was left lying there on the living room floor, my eyes wide open, staring at the ceiling. My soul was cleansed. My mind was free. My heart was open.

I had forgiven my father.

With the Holy Spirit's power and help, I was released from the animosity, the bitterness, the anger, the hatred that had been bottled up inside for most, if not all, of my life. The unforgiveness I had carried around for decades was a chain dragging me down, keeping me locked up and entangled with all of my father's failings. Forgiveness broke that chain. I had thought that, if I forgave him, he would benefit from it. But in that moment, I was the one receiving the blessing of my forgiveness.

I felt a burden lifted that I had carried far too long. By forgiving my father, I let go of that one thing that had kept me from being at peace with myself, at peace with my God, and at peace with the world around me. There was a spiritual power coursing through me, like a baptism, that translated into love, into joy, into a new beginning.

Once I was finally able to get up from the living room floor, I went in and woke Heather to tell her what had happened. We hugged, and cried, and then we pretty much forgot about it. At the time, I gave no thought to contacting my father to tell him. Because of that last experience, just a few months before when I delivered the divorce papers, I had no hope of him changing. He was as he had always been. Could God change him? Of course. But I didn't think that my telling him I had forgiven him would bring about that change.

As far as I was concerned, what happened that night in the living room of our two-bedroom apartment was a personal matter. I kept the story to myself. For at least sixteen more years, my father and I had no relationship at all.

During that time, Heather saw my father twice; once at my grandmother's ninetieth birthday party. There was no interaction, beyond what might have been a polite hello and goodbye, mainly out of respect for my grandmother. And the second was at my grandmother's funeral. Again, nothing beyond my saying that I was sorry for his loss—something you might say to a person you barely knew from work or the neighborhood. After the service, we all went to a diner to spend some time celebrating my grandmother's life and to reminisce. It was weird, having him sit across from us at a small table. He seemed nervous. He didn't know us, and he showed no interest in getting to know us.

By this time, we had our two boys. He asked nothing about them. He had never met (and still hasn't) his two grandsons, and he had nothing to say to his son and daughter-in-law about them. I had to remind myself that I had forgiven him.

I thought forgiveness was a one and done deal.

But the Lord wasn't finished with me on that subject. I saw that, just as I have to continue going to my heavenly Father to ask for his forgiveness, I needed to continue going to my heavenly Father to ask his help forgiving my earthly father. The pain of the past would rear its ugly head and bring back all of those things that had been set free that night in our living room.

I started to consider that perhaps I should tell him the story. Let him know directly that I had forgiven him. Whether it was wisdom or cowardice, I'm not sure, but I decided to write him a letter rather than telling him in person. I wrote down the story of what happened that night, basically as I told it above, and then I spelled it out.

I forgive you. I hope you've found God.

I mailed the letter. For weeks I heard nothing. No response.

I also began to wonder if there was anything that I had done that I needed to ask for his forgiveness. Things like:

Calling him out in front of my uncle that day at my grandparents' house.

Wadding up the hundred-dollar bill and throwing it in the trash can.

*Hand-delivering the divorce papers myself rather than
having someone else do it.*

On a Monday afternoon between clients, I jumped on my
bike and rode down to Times Square to see the Erwin Brothers'
film, *I Can Only Imagine*. It's a true story of the very difficult
relationship the lead singer for the band MercyMe had with his
abusive father. I saw so much of my own experience in his. I left
the theater in tears and yet with hope. They were able to recon-
cile, to make things right with each other.

Finally, I decided to call my father to schedule a meeting.

I had a knot in my stomach and secretly hoped that he
wouldn't answer.

He took my call.

When I asked if he had gotten my letter, rather than
graciously accepting my forgiving him, he blasted what I had
written. He said that of course he knew God—he had taught
Sunday School!

I told him again the purpose of my call, and I asked if
perhaps we could meet in person to talk about it. He quoted
a couple of Bible verses at me, said he was leaving the next day
for China, and that he would call me when he got back.

I decided to take it one step further. I asked him if there
was anything that I had done to him that needed his forgiveness. In one of the few moments of normalcy in a father/son
relationship of over forty years, he said this:

"Danny, you did nothing wrong. You're a good kid. There's
nothing I need to forgive you for."

We hung up from that phone call and have only spoken a
couple of times since, also by phone. As far as I know, he's back
in China, where he has a girlfriend.

I've told this story several times publicly. A church dinner
talk I gave was recorded, and I shared it with my mom and

siblings. I met with Mom at a Brooklyn diner to talk about it. I longed for her to experience the same freedom I had in letting go, in being set free from what I had held onto against my father.

As I told her what happened with me, her eyes welled up with tears. She told me that she also had forgiven him, but that she doesn't ever want to see him again. The man made her life a living Hell. The fact that she was even able to say the words, "I forgive him," was proof to me of the power of God. And it also spoke volumes about the loving, gentle soul—my hero—who sat across the table from me.

From my own experience, I believe that the chains of unforgiveness are always lurking, always looking for an opportunity to wrap us again in the hurt and anger we feel toward the one who offended us. If we allow those chains, they will bury us in bitterness. Forgiveness, even if it means doing it over and over and over again, is the only way to break those chains and truly be set free.

You should know—while writing this chapter and thinking again about all of his offenses, they have tried to entrap me once again.

So, with that, I say to my father:

I have forgiven you.
I am forgiving you.
I will forgive you.

I pray that he, too, will find peace with God.

Brooklyn, 1974: John, 10, my mom, me, 3, on my father's lap,
James, 6, and Janet, 9.

Our Lady of Angels schoolyard, 1978:
Where the dream began at seven years old.

Senior year at Fort Hamilton High School, 1989

My scout, Herb Stein, and a proud new member of the Twins.

My mom and me after one of my games in Elizabethton, Tennessee.

Fort Wayne's Danny Venezia leaps over George Williams and fires to first Wednesday night.

Turning two against the Oakland A's affiliate, the West Michigan Whitecaps.

Me and my best bud, Joe, before our speech at McKinley Junior High, 1993.

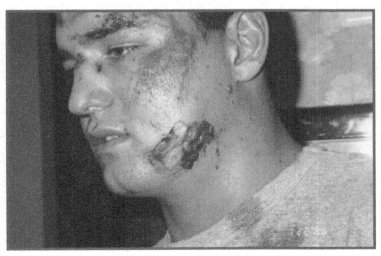

September, 1994—After the head-on collision. This was my first bout with a near-death experience.

The two boys I saw in my near-death vision,
fourteen years before this picture was taken.

My one and only true love!

October 2, 1998—Two have become one!

My father-in-law and me taking a well-deserved break while building my home.

Ryan and Skyler. May the peace of the Lord be with them always.

Blessed are those who see God through the eyes of a child.
Ryan (top right) and Skyler (bottom left).

One of my favorite pics of all time. Your kids are always watching!

Just another day in the ballpark with Ryan and Skyler.

Vacationing in Cancun.

John, James, Janet, and me with our hero at the center.

My first retreat—Men's Cornerstone 15.

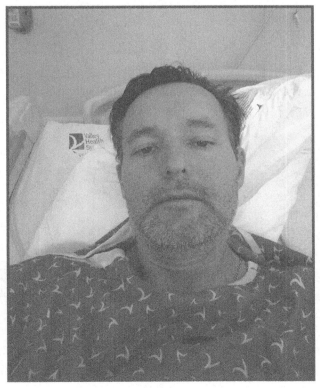

In the hospital battling COVID-19.

Monsignor Geno and me at The Cathedral of St. John the Baptist,
Paterson, New Jersey.

Heather's fiftieth birthday party, March 2019. This is also the picture that
helped get me through my hospital stay.

No description necessary.

CHAPTER NINE

A FATHER'S GUIDANCE

He showed me how to build a house. Along the way, he taught me how to build a home.

Paul Englehardt often told me that I had hit the lottery by landing Heather. He was right—but my winnings didn't stop with the love of my life. With Heather, I got the Powerball—her family, with its head, my new father-in-law.

I wasn't sure what our relationship would be like when we first met. It was around three in the afternoon on a Saturday, and Heather had taken me to his home to introduce me.

"What can I get you to drink?" he asked.

I didn't think that asking for a gin martini would be a good impression to make on the man whose daughter I hoped to marry, so I played it safe.

"Iced tea would be great."

"I meant an adult beverage. There's the fridge. You can get it yourself."

Wow. *This guy's tough as nails*, I thought.

Determined to do better, I offered to help him with some work he was doing in the kitchen. He was preparing to paint, and he needed to repair some holes and cracks in the walls.

"Can you spackle?"

"Sure."

I had never spackled in my life.

He took me out into his massive garage, and I thought I had just walked into The Home Depot. He had every tool imaginable—compressors, nail guns, table saws, generators. I found out later that if he didn't have the tool he needed, and the best one to get the job done, he was more than happy to run right out and add that one to his arsenal.

Growing up in Brooklyn apartments all of my life, the only tools I had ever used were the few that could fit in the junk drawer of a kitchenette. Handling a small hammer, a pair of pliers, and a Phillips or flat-head screwdriver was about the extent of my tool experience.

He handed me a galvanized mud pan with a heaping scoop of drywall compound, along with a spackling knife. Not at all knowing what I was doing, I took the edge of the knife, got just a tiny bit of the compound on it, and tried to push it into the places needing repair. I wanted to be careful and not get spackle anywhere but in the crack itself. No doubt he was cracking up inside, watching and laughing at my ineptitude. But he said nothing.

The next day, Heather took me back to her father's house. The cracks and holes in the kitchen, which I had so pitifully tried to repair, were covered, sanded, and ready for a fresh coat of paint. I learned a lot about the man who would become my father-in-law that weekend in the kitchen—he was tough, telling me to get my own iced tea, but also kind; he covered up my horrible spackling job without embarrassing me or calling me out.

Having driven and worked on tanks during the Korean War, Mr. E, as I eventually came to call him, could fix just about anything. And if he couldn't fix it, he would make it.

Over the course of his life, he was an inventor, owned a body shop, and served as a pilot and a flight instructor (at one point he owned eight airplanes and would have built his own airport if Heather's mom hadn't objected). He also was an insurance adjuster and a landlord who handled all of the repairs on his rental properties. At one point, he owned eight businesses with over one hundred people working for him. I would be willing to bet that he knew every one of them by name and could talk with you about each of their families.

He was the most generous man I ever met. But it was never to draw attention to himself—he lived, through his actions, the command of Jesus—*love your neighbor as yourself.* He would buy drinks for strangers in restaurants, pick up the tab for his friends; he gave anonymously to many organizations; he took the entire eighth grade from Heather's middle school to his Canadian vacation home; and he allowed a stranger to borrow his backhoe—worth a small fortune and equipped with a full tank of gas—handing him the keys without asking any questions.

I became the recipient of that generosity about two years into our marriage. On one of our Sunday afternoons at his home, I remember complimenting him on how beautiful everything was. The landscaping, the pool, the tennis court—for kids, living there would have been like always being away at summer camp. There was volleyball, basketball, a game room, and a movie room in the basement. Heather grew up with all of this, and a dad who would fly the family in one of his planes to the Caribbean for vacation.

My vacations were spent at the island surrounding the fire hydrant on our Brooklyn block, using a vegetable can with holes punched in it, which we would take turns holding over the water gushing out, to create our own sprinkler. Of course that wasn't legal—if the police showed up, we would scatter, climbing fences and running down alleys until the coast was clear.

The differences in our childhoods didn't seem to bother Heather or her dad. He also grew up with little, earning everything he had by hard work and determination. One of his favorite sayings, which he repeated often while enjoying a good meal and his favorite drink, Southern Comfort, was:

The meal at the end of the day, along with an adult beverage, tastes a lot better after putting in a solid day's work.

So, the day that I complimented him on his home, I was dreaming of future memories, of my future family, and what I would be able to offer them. I didn't realize at the time how closely he was listening to me. Or that he was putting together a plan to help me fulfill my dreams.

As I mentioned earlier, for the first two years of our marriage we rented an apartment and saved Heather's salary to buy a house. We had also saved the very generous monetary gifts we received at our wedding. We did splurge on our honeymoon to Europe, but I paid for that with practically every penny I had managed to save up to that point in my life. When Heather's dad found out that we had saved our wedding gift money and Heather's salary for a house, he was very excited.

We were at his favorite restaurant, Ossy's Café in Hawthorne. It was one of those nights that he bought drinks for strangers and picked up the tabs of his acquaintances.

"Danny, it's not how you start, it's how you finish," he said after ordering another round of drinks.

At that time, I was just leaving my job as the manager and trainer at a fitness training facility in Manhattan to start my own business. He continued.

"If what you're doing isn't working, don't ever be afraid to try something else."

I can't tell you how freeing it was to hear that from this man who had lived the American Dream, whose own entrepreneurial spirit had lifted him to the heights of success. It took a lot of the pressure off needing to make this one thing successful. And then he said the words that every son would want to hear from his father:

"Danny, I'm not worried about you. You will be there at the finish line."

I fought back tears. From my college years studying psychology, I learned that every young man needs three A's from his father—*Affection, Attention, and Approval.* Having never received any of the three from my biological father, there was a hole in my soul that this man, who could fix anything, stepped in to fill. He spackled my heart. When he spoke those words to me with a gleam in his eye (and even if it was after perhaps one too many adult beverages), I received the approval, the attention, and the affection I longed for from my father.

Once he learned that we had saved all that money and were ready to look for a house, he went to work to help us. We had found a couple of places we were interested in, but each of those fell through. One day while I was at work in the city, he took Heather to see a small bungalow about ten feet off the road in North Haledon. It had more property than any other house on the street—it actually sat on two lots—with one hundred feet of frontage and running a full football field deep.

At first, Heather refused to even get out of the car. She said that the house was so old and scary she couldn't imagine what her dad was thinking. But he was envisioning what the place could be with a little hard work.

Okay, maybe a lot of hard work.

But that never scared him away from a project.

Nor me. My years of working harder than everyone else at baseball prepared me for what I was about to embark on with Mr. E. At first, he and I planned to renovate the house already on the property. But once Heather and I agreed to buy it, after some negotiation she won the battle to tear down the existing structure and start all over.

We were going to build our own home from the ground up.

He began by buying that backhoe I mentioned earlier. He cleared out trees and underbrush, and we started to see the potential he had seen for our future home. He named our new family "business" B, B & B Construction—Brains, Brawn, and Beauty. It shouldn't take anyone very long to figure out who was who. He had the vision and the know-how, I had the young, strong back (at least among the three of us), and Heather is definitely beautiful!

That being said, she played her part in the construction as well. He may have had six daughters, but he often treated them like sons, teaching them to do things around the house that I had never learned. Heather sanded and stained every piece of molding, spindle, and door. She was up on the scaffolding helping with the siding and the roof. She brought much more than her beauty to our enterprise.

Because almost all of our savings had gone into buying the property, Heather and I moved in with her sister Kristen and her husband, Matt. To pay rent, the construction loan, and the mortgage payment would have really stretched our already tight budget. Heather and I will never forget their generosity in welcoming us.

I did my work in the city from noon until 7:00 p.m., but I was working eighteen to twenty-hour days—up every morning at 4:30 a.m., at the property by 5, working on the house until 10:30, then showering and heading off to the city to be at work at noon. At 7, I would head back to the property to work until 10 or 11 p.m., get a few hours of sleep, and then do it all over again the next day. And I loved it! Most days, anyway.

I started by helping demolish and remove the old structure on the property. We didn't want to incur the cost of a dumpster, which was way too expensive, so we took advantage of the "entrepreneurs," as Mr. E called them. Over a two-month period, the garbage men carried away the entire house—and a chicken coop. I quickly learned how to use Mr. E's compound saw, which I still have. I believe that he inherited it from his father or grandfather. Trust me, as heavy and solid as this thing is, it should last an eternity. I threw out my herniated L4 and L5 discs, the ones injured in the accident, several times just carrying the darn thing.

Piece-by-piece I chopped the chicken coop up into five-foot sections and tied them into bundles. We could put about ten of them out at a time, and off they went. After scraping off the roof shingles, we began to cut the house down, trying first with the chainsaw. "Brains" decided that the reciprocal saw worked best, and a dozen blades later, we were down to the first level.

From there I gutted the walls with crowbars and sledgehammers. It was messy grunt work, but so satisfying to see it go. I was learning, in reverse, what goes where when building a home. Every time I opened a wall, I envisioned a mouse or rat coming out. There were droppings everywhere. I also dreamed of finding a pile of cash hidden away. Gladly I didn't encounter any rodents, and sadly I never found a treasure chest.

When our new "business partners" threw the bathtub and the front metal porch gate in the back of their truck, we knew we were in good shape. We had closed on the property in October. By Christmas, sixteen garbage truck loads had carried away everything but the front wall. We hung a wreath on it to celebrate.

Mr. E was a great teacher. And I turned out to be a pretty good apprentice. For the next fifteen years or so, he loved to say to anyone willing to listen, "You know, before I got him, Danny couldn't hold a hammer."

Speaking of hammers, when I first started putting the sheathing up on the side of the house, I was wearing a belt and using a fancy nail gun. The next day, Brains came over to check out Brawn's work. He showed me all the nails I put in that had missed the studs—at least half. He explained that this created two problems—one, the house wouldn't pass inspection like that, and two, even if it did pass inspection, it would soon fall apart.

He made me hand over the nail gun and gave me a bag of nails and a red hammer, one that I still have and use today. Every time I pick it up, I remember the lesson he taught me that day. I learned the sound that a nail gun makes when it misses the stud—indistinct, and easy to miss. But with a hammer and a nail, you know immediately whether or not you've hit your mark. When you miss, you pry it out and try again to drive it home. With the same concentration, preparation, and motivation I used to drive in runs on the baseball field, I drove in those nails, this time to build a house that would become a home for my family.

Mr. E was proud of the work we did together. I grew more and more confident, thriving under his tutelage and encouragement—except for the heights. Mr. E was sixty-seven when we built the house. I wanted to do all the heavy lifting and climbing of ladders, despite my deadly fear of heights. I had a lot of nightmares during the time we worked on the second story and roof.

One ladder experience was especially costly. I had one more piece of sheathing left to put up on the right side of the house. I needed Mr. E's help, so he leaned out of the second story bathroom window as I slid the large piece of plywood up the ladder. Four feet by eight feet pieces of plywood are not easy to manage by yourself. Like always, my knees started shaking when I got above ten feet high. They shook even more when Mr. E. yelled at me.

"What the hell is this? This is three-quarter-inch wood! That's for the roof!"

My mistake of using roofing plywood for the side of the house cost Heather and me $800. Mr. E eventually got his money's worth out of it, razzing me, laughing, and telling the story to Heather over and over while enjoying a couple of his adult beverages. He never held anything against me. He spoke his mind if he thought something was wrong, but once said, it was in the past, over. I joined in and laughed at myself. I told them that if we had a tornado or hurricane (which rarely happens in our area of New Jersey), we could nestle in and know we were safe on that side of the house.

Much later, I was running electric wire underground to my backyard shed. By this time, I was confident that I had developed my skills as an electrician. Suddenly, there were a couple of sparks, and the power went out. Not just at our house, but all over town. I thought I had done something to cause the power outage. When Mr. E heard the story, he got a big laugh out of that one. He gave me a new nickname—"Sparky." Now, when I go to Ossy's with my family, the owners and waiters still call me by that nickname. Some of those really stick.

As we made progress on the house, every time I finished one job, he taught me how to use a new tool and set me up for the next one. I ran every piece of wire and put in almost every outlet, light, and light switch, while he moved on to build the kitchen counter, the staircase, or put in the plumbing fixtures. My brother-in-law, Joe, a carpenter by trade at the time, had come over with his friends, and in two weekends they framed the entire house. I put up all of the drywall, and Mr. E spackled every seam and every hole. I guess he still didn't trust me with that job.

When he took a break from our house to go do some work on one of his other daughters' homes, I took the opportunity to show him what I'd learned. I finished our basement. I framed the walls, ran the electric, sheet rocked, put in the drop ceiling—but I waited for him to return for the spackle. I did it partly as a joke, but also to let him know I still needed him. He was my mentor, and nobody could spackle like Mr. E!

On Heather's birthday, which was a Sunday that year, I wanted to surprise her by having family and friends over. The kitchen cabinets were in, but the floor tile wasn't down yet. Mr. E agreed to work all day Saturday and make it happen. Nineteen hours later, around 3 a.m., the job was done. Only the two of us ever knew the imperfections in our work after several adult beverages during the evening—as parents like to say, nothing good ever happens after midnight!

Other than pouring concrete and Mr. E's friend doing all the roughing in of the plumbing, we did everything. There was an overabundance of sweat equity in the house that became a home for the Venezias. After a year's worth of work, Heather and I moved in. Only the downstairs and our bedroom were finished, but we eagerly started to settle in. We continued to work on the remaining bedrooms over the next few months.

When I had learned all of his lessons and finished the inside of the house, he told me I should work on the cabana. We had decided to go ahead and put a pool in the backyard. Of course, a pool needs a cabana—we planned for one about twenty by ten feet. I needed to frame a spot for a bathroom, a changing room, and the rest for the pool filter. He trusted me to do it all on my own now. The master released the apprentice to do the work by himself. Of course, he was always a phone call or car trip away if I needed him.

If I hit a snag as I did that work, rather than immediately picking up the phone and asking him a question or to come right over, I would stop and try to think like Mr. E.

What would he say?

What would he do?

Many times, that strategy worked. When it didn't, I still had my ace in the hole, who would always be there for me if I needed him.

One of the best lessons he taught me was to allow myself to make mistakes. He would say:

"Experience is a long list of mistakes."

I would joke with him, saying, "Oh, okay, so it's not just me. You've made this mistake before too!"

Mr. E would smile and say, "More than once."

I still haven't heard a better definition of experience than this in my lifetime. It's worth repeating:

"Experience is a long list of mistakes."

That year with Paul Englehardt—Mr. E, Mr. Mayor, Bud, Buddy, Pops, Dad—was special in so many ways. Here was a role model for me as a father and provider. I wanted to prove him right, to fulfill his words of affirmation—to be there at the finish line.

Our apartment in West Paterson was only a mile from the cemetery where Heather's mom was laid to rest. Early in our marriage, before we started working on the house, I would visit there, often with a flower to put at her resting place. Somehow I felt a connection to the mother-in-law I never met. Standing there, I would assure her that she'd done a great job raising her daughters and that Heather was in good hands. One day, during one of these visits, Mr. E walked up. I don't remember what was said—he didn't ask why I was there. I know that we shared some small talk and then I let him have his time. He never brought it up to Heather. He didn't need to know why I was there. My gut tells me that it didn't matter—the simple fact that I was there was enough for him. I believe that's one of the reasons he thought I would be there at the finish line.

I said at the beginning of this chapter that he showed me how to build a house, but he taught me how to build a home. If his cell phone rang while we were working, even if he was up on a ladder or in the middle of something, when he saw it was one of his six daughters or nineteen grandchildren, he always took the call. He would get down from the ladder or stop whatever he was doing to devote his full attention to the person on the other end of that line. And if he needed to, he would go do whatever they needed and come back later to finish our job.

I remember asking his advice about our mortgage payments one day. I had heard that if I made one extra principal payment a year, I could cut years off the length of the mortgage.

"Danny," he said, "take that money and go on vacation. Thirty years go by in a blink! Invest that money in time away with your family. You'll never regret that investment."

This was the connecting place for family, from the Venn diagram the investigator had drawn at my mom's kitchen table.

From his grandfather, Mr. E taught me:

"Never cry over money lost. Figure out a way to make more."

He saw America as the one place in the world where everyone had the opportunity to do just that. This was the American Dream his grandfather had left Germany to pursue. He had a thirty-foot flagpole in his front yard, and he was always buying a bigger flag to replace the one he had. At eighteen, he volunteered to go into the army during a time of war. In Korea, where he worked in the tank division, he was promoted to Sergeant First Class. He received a Korean War medal, a United Nations award, and a bronze star for his two years of service on the front lines. He served his community on the Board of Education and as Mayor of Hawthorne.

At eighty-three, squamous cell cancer was taking its toll. After dozens of chemotherapy and radiation treatments, he underwent a fourteen-hour surgery. They had to take a piece of his thigh and attach it to his skull. Although the medical team didn't think he would ever walk again, soon after that surgery he asked to go to Ryan and Skyler's basketball game. We found a place in the corner of St. Anthony's gymnasium where he could have a clear line of sight from his wheelchair. Before the game began, as they played the National Anthem, we watched in amazement as he struggled to stand at attention and salute the flag of the country he loved.

After that same surgery, for a time, he lost the ability to breathe on his own. The doctors brought him back, and he brought us back a story of Heaven. He told us that he briefly went to a place where he was free from pain—a place of peace and tranquility. After that, he wore a cross outside of his shirt instead of hidden away.

He liked to say that he had six daughters, eight businesses, and nine lives. He survived the ravages of war in Korea, an earthquake in Taiwan, falling off a ladder at his body shop, several plane crashes, and landing on a dirt road in the Bahamas after running out of fuel. But the years progressed, and eventually time and that insidious cancer did what nothing else could to Paul Englehardt.

I received the honor of giving the eulogy for the man I came to love as a father. I thank God that I had the opportunity to know him, to become a part of his family, to thank him for the love and care he gave me, and to tell him that I loved him.

My biological father taught me, by example, *what I did not want to be* as a father. My father-in-law taught me, by example, *what I could be* as a father. He never tried to tell me anything that I didn't see him living out—in the way he dealt with his family, in the way he dealt with other people, in the way he dealt with life.

I don't believe there is anything that needs to be fixed in Heaven. But if there is, God has one heavenly handyman.

And so I say—

Godspeed, Mr. E—

Dad—

Until we meet again.

CHAPTER TEN

BECOMING A FATHER

Heather and I had been in our new home for about a year and a half when our first son, Ryan, was born. Less than a year and a half later, our second son, Skyler, came along. It didn't take long to figure out that being the father I want to be requires just as much, if not more, of the focus, concentration, and commitment I had to use as a professional athlete and an amateur construction worker. When we were building our home, Mr. E asked me one day, "What's the difference between a professional and an amateur?" His answer—"Professionals get paid."

When Ryan was first born, and we were still at the hospital, he wouldn't stop crying when we were wheeling his bassinet back down to the baby station. I leaned over and spoke to him.

"It's okay, Buddy. Daddy is here."

He stopped crying immediately. I knew then that all those nights I had spoken to him during Heather's pregnancy had helped him recognize my voice. I learned a spiritual lesson as well—I need to listen for, and learn to respond immediately, to my Heavenly Father's voice.

While Heather was pregnant with Ryan, he seemed quite comfortable there, never making much of a fuss. With Skyler, it was a totally different experience. Knuckles and knees and feet were constantly pushing against Heather's skin—it looked like there was a fight going on inside her. That child wanted out of there, and fast! Now we can see that, even in the womb, their personalities were at play.

When the boys were little, they went through a time when it seemed like they were always screaming at each other. It really bothered Heather and me—we sat down together to try to figure out why it was happening and what we should do. Were they learning it from other kids they were around? From the television shows they were watching? I was convinced it was that awful, screaming sea monster, "SpongeBob SquarePants."

After one particularly loud shouting match, I'd had enough. "Okay, boys. NO MORE TELEVISION!"

I said it loudly to make my point.

Within five minutes, they were at it again.

"STOP YOUR SCREAMING!" I screamed.

I looked at Heather. She looked at me. We both knew in that moment where the boys were learning their behavior. They got it from me. I had been raising my voice at them much too often. Lesson—scream at your children, and you raise screamers.

I stopped. And soon, so did they.

When the boys were around two and three, we were invited out to California to celebrate Heather's sister Caryn's fortieth birthday. Heather wanted to take the boys to Disneyland while we were there. At first, I said no. I thought we should wait until they were older and could remember more about the trip. Thankfully, Heather won that debate and proved me wrong (like she does a lot!).

I can't put into words the feeling I had as a father, looking at my sons' eyes as they experienced that fantasyland world. "Pirates of the Caribbean," "Peter Pan," and "It's a Small World" took on a whole new meaning for me as I watched them, mesmerized as they were by the wonder of it all. Pure joy illuminated their faces. I learned again on that trip—allow every moment to count! Don't put off for some possible future tomorrow the memories you can make today.

Not every magical moment has to come at a Disney park. Moments of introduction, their first times experiencing even the littlest things, can be just as magical. What can be better than teaching your sons how to eat an Oreo cookie? (And as far as I'm concerned, there's only one way!) They've never forgotten that one.

Like a lot of houses, ours had what many call a formal dining room. For the first few years, we only used it for Thanksgiving and Christmas dinner. The rest of the time it may have looked pretty, but it went unused. I decided that needed to change.

Growing up, I remember going to our relatives' houses and seeing plastic on their furniture. I learned that it was there to keep us kids from ruining it. I can still feel and hear the crunch when I sat down. Now Heather and I were basically doing the same thing. We didn't have plastic on the chairs, but by almost never using the room, we were delivering the same message. I asked Heather, "What good is the nice dining room set if we don't have any memories to go with it?"

Together, we made the decision to have Sunday night dinner in our dining room. It's a tradition we continue today. As soon as the boys were old enough, they started helping me mix and roll the meatballs and make homemade garlic bread. When we get home from church, we put the pot of sauce on. Doing this on Sundays gives Mom a day off from the kitchen.

If you come to our house for Sunday dinner now, you'll likely see spaghetti stains on the dining room chairs. Sure, they would be much cleaner if we had plastic on them or only used them for Thanksgiving and Christmas. But creating the memories we share from those times around that table are priceless compared to keeping our stuff in pristine condition. With young boys (and probably young girls too), marinara will sometimes spill from their fork onto a chair—but trust me, what spills from their mouths is worth ever so much more.

Not only did we start the tradition of having Sunday dinner in the dining room, we still try to have dinner together every night. When the boys were younger, on Taco Tuesdays, they got to smash up a bag of Doritos and then put the rest of the ingredients in the bag and shake it up. Every Friday night was "Pizza and a Movie" night—sometimes we let the kids make their own. We would lay a blanket out in the family room in front of the TV, and the boys alternated picking the movie.

And like I learned at my aunt and uncle's house, we use that same blessing before our meals at the dinner table:

Thank you, dear Lord, for this food we're about to receive.
Thank you for all the blessings you've given us. Help
anyone who needs our prayers.

Then we add the names of those who need prayer—a friend who's hurting, a relative who's sick, our national or local leaders in a time of trouble.

Heather has done an awesome job of making sure we have dinner together every night, especially when my schedule keeps me in the city late. The meal itself is far less important than the conversations we have during it. We listen to find out about what's gone on during their day. Our boys are free to discuss their feelings, their thoughts, their creative ideas—early on we decided that no subject was off limits.

Except for one thing—gossip is never allowed. We try to enforce that rule at all times. And trust me, it is just as hard, or harder, for Heather and me as it is for our two boys. This didn't mean that they couldn't tell us if "so and so" took their pencil or was being mean to them. We needed to hear that so we could help them work through issues at school. Hideki Matsui, who played for years with the Yankees, wrote a book on character, *Sportsmanship, Modesty, and the Art of the Home Run*. He told the story of telling a group of reporters that he had never said a bad word about anyone. When they challenged him, "Never?!"

He said, "I didn't say I never thought it. I just never said it."

That's the lesson we wanted our boys to learn. What we didn't allow was hearing someone called a "jerk" or "stupid." Maybe they'd done something and were acting that way—but Heather and I took the approach that maybe they were just having a bad day. Give them another chance. We wanted to teach the boys to always try and put themselves in the other person's shoes before making a judgment about them.

I knew that lesson was sinking in while coaching one of my sons' youth baseball games. With our team in the field, one of our outfielders made an error that cost our team a couple of runs. He was clearly upset about it—he felt horrible. With our team at bat, I had to leave the dugout to coach third base. The young boy's father, my friend, George, was coming over to our dugout to comfort his son. As he walked up, he heard one of our players say to his son, "You know we're losing because you missed that ball!"

Before George could say anything, my oldest, Ryan, put his arm around our right fielder.

"You didn't miss that ball. *We* did. Now come on, let's win this!"

George turned around and went back to the bleachers. And by the way—we did come back and win. But winning the game wasn't the important thing that happened on the field that day. Teamwork, compassion, friendship happened—and I believe that even the player who initially said the wrong thing learned a lesson too. Seeing our kids win at life is always much better and more rewarding than what the scoreboard may show at the end of a game.

My youngest, Skyler, taught me a lesson on the baseball field when he was four years old. The two of us had gone out to work on his hitting and fielding. I brought a bucket of balls, our gloves, and a tiny t-ball bat. I put down a portable pitching rubber at a reasonable distance from home plate for someone his age. Four-year-olds don't typically pitch—we usually don't start them until they're eight, and even then they have trouble getting the ball consistently over the plate. But Skyler had shown an interest in pitching, and I was more than willing to work with him.

After throwing about a dozen balls from the portable rubber, Skyler got bored with that distance. He proceeded to march back sixty feet, six inches to the field's actual pitching mound, the distance that big league pitchers pitch from.

"Where do you think you're going?" I asked.

"To the real pitching mound. I want to pitch from there."

"Skyler, you can't do that. It's too far away."

Remember the lesson I learned from Mr. E?

Experience is a long list of mistakes.

With that comment, I added to my already long list, gaining some parenting experience.

Skyler gave me a look. I recognized it immediately. I've seen that same look from his mother—just a few times, thankfully, but enough to know what it meant.

He got on the mound and threw three straight strikes. On a straight line.

My three-foot-tall, thirty-five-pound, hurling four-year-old caught the attention of several teenagers who were riding their bikes at the field. He knew they were watching, and he naturally felt good about himself and his performance. As they rode off, he said in a low voice that only I could hear, "I can whistle, too."

He pressed those little lips together, blowing over and over, until finally a subtle sound came out. He looked at me and smiled. Humbled and proud, I smiled back.

Skyler taught me two lessons that day. First, that I *could* learn a lesson from my four-year-old son. Second, never say "can't." We really don't know what we, or our children, might be able to accomplish if we simply try.

When my sons were in the "my dad can do anything" stage, I was Superman. The boys would run to the door when I arrived home from work. I would pick them up and fly them around the house, putting my arms under their chests and legs. With their arms stretched straight out, our kitchen became the Great Wall of China, our foyer the Eiffel Tower, and we would crash land in the Grand Canyon (our family room) to wrestle on the floor like a tiger with his cubs.

We would settle in for a game of chess until it was time for bed and a story. We read their favorites, like C.S. Lewis's *The Lion, the Witch, and the Wardrobe* and Mark Twain's *Huckleberry Finn*, or I would make up my own stories about Sir Ryan and Sir Skyler, knights sent to rescue the beautiful princess (their mom) from the evil king in the castle.

In those early years, I had a captivated audience. They soaked up everything I could teach them, eager to learn, wanting to rip off their diapers, then the training wheels on their bikes, then the book out of my hand so they could read on their own. Those were miraculous days with the two miracles God had given Heather and me.

I especially remember going shopping with the boys at the bagel store. We had a deal—if they could figure out what the change would be, before the cashier could do it on the register, then they got to keep the change (coins, not bills). They got good at adding and subtracting at a very young age, eventually beating the machine every single time. Now, they're both really good with numbers. I don't doubt this helped accelerate the process.

It also reinforced for me that incentives are good. We talked about fractions and percentages well before they learned it in school. If we were out to eat as a family on Saturday night, Ryan would take the check at age five and calculate the tip. Skyler applied his problem solving and money-making in more creative ways.

One day I went into the garage and found him using duct tape to secure a nail to a broom handle.

"Skyler, what are you doing? Spear fishing?"

He explained that he had spotted a wad of money down a drain on the side of the road near the school. Meanwhile, his older brother had come out, heard the story, and wanted a piece of the action. The three of us got on our bikes and rode down to where he had seen the cash. I thought it best that I carry his handmade spear. Once we got to the drain, Skyler's invention worked like a charm—he stabbed the bills and brought them up slowly, and Ryan was there to grab them before they fell back to the bottom. When the boys were seven dollars richer, there was still one more dollar bill that Skyler just couldn't get to stick on the nail, which was blunted from hitting the concrete over and over.

Nonplussed, he handed me the tool and asked me to hold it for a second. He calmly took a piece of gum out of his pocket, chewed it, then took it out of his mouth and stuck it on the end of the nail. In no time, he'd successfully navigated the last dollar bill out of the drain. With eight bucks to his credit, he decided to share three of them with his brother. I was duly impressed.

We worked at teaching the boys the importance of giving an offering at church. One Sunday, Ryan had his dollar ready, I thought, but when the collection basket passed, he didn't put it in. Before we left church, I questioned him about it.

"Ryan, why didn't you put your money in the basket?"

"Then I wouldn't have it anymore."

"You can always make more money."

"How?"

We came up with a business plan—*Ryan's Lemonade Stand*. Before we left church that day, he took his dollar and put it in the box at the back for the poor. At six years old, he was excited about becoming an entrepreneur.

We talked about the cost of doing business and finding an initial investor—me. I would help him get started by buying cups and lemons (his mom donated the sugar). I explained that once he recouped those initial costs, he would start making a profit. Before he set up his stand on the sidewalk, he gave me $4.75 in change from his piggy bank.

"Here, Dad. Now I don't owe you anything."

He paid off his initial investor before making a cent on his product. After that, he never hesitated to put his money in the church basket.

When the boys were eight and nine, they were on the same football team. Heather and I were going to buy them football jackets with their team's name on the back. Ryan stopped me.

"Dad, if we win the Super Bowl, we get them for free!"

I loved his confidence.

As one of the younger kids on the team, Skyler didn't start every game. I wondered why. Over two seasons, he had only dropped one pass that was thrown to him, and that was the very first one that came his way. After not playing for several weeks, he started walking around the house with the football in his hands. He even took it to bed with him. I asked why.

"When I get my chance, I don't want to drop it again," he said.

Then he really floored me.

"Dad, can you throw me some passes in the yard after school?"

I only hated that he had to ask!

"You bet. As soon as you finish your homework."

Every day, we were in the backyard, and I would throw him one hundred passes.

"Dad, you've gotta make me dive. Don't throw them so perfect!"

I did. They made it to the playoffs, and Skyler got to play in the semi-final. After a touchdown, the quarterback threw the ball to Skyler in the end zone for the extra point. The ball stuck like glue to those well-practiced little hands. They won!

Which meant they made it to the Super Bowl. As regulation time was running out, Skyler caught the game-tying touchdown pass. Then, in overtime, he made a one-handed catch in the back of the end zone, keeping both feet in bounds, just like we had practiced hundreds of times in the backyard. Their team won the Super Bowl, and they got their free but well-earned jackets.

I never let my boys win at anything. Cards, chess, one-on-one basketball, races—they learned that each victory had to be won by effort. During a chess game, when they were learning, I would make some wrong moves to keep the game going and get them to see a few steps ahead. Clearly I taught him well—Ryan won't play me anymore, because it's no longer a challenge. The same is true for one-on-one basketball with Skyler—Dad can no longer keep up. Competition is good, in the right context. Even more than winning, I wanted them to learn to play the game right!

I made sure that no matter how tired I was after a long day at work, I was always willing to say "yes" to their requests:

Dad, will you help me with my homework?
Dad, will you read me a story?
Dad, will you play catch with me?
Dad, how about a game of one-on-one?

But I never pushed them. Even now, the desire has to come from them. It has to be their passion—their dreams belong to them. When it came to sports, it was all about their effort and attitude. Playing baseball, my sons had a slight edge—not only with nature but nurture. They learned the game at a young age from someone who played at a high level.

Skyler retired from baseball at age twelve—he decided that basketball was his game. And he works hard at it—on the asphalt in our driveway, in the workout facility, and on the gym floor. I believe, and I teach my sons, that it's the climb, it's the battle, that matters.

When Ryan was around twelve, one of his baseball games went eleven innings. The umpire finally called it a tie because it was a school night. During the game, Ryan pitched a gem and was called a bulldog by one of the parents after diving for a ball in foul territory, inches from the fence. In his room as he was going to bed, Ryan told me he'd been up a specific number of hours. I did the math—his numbers didn't add up.

Heather showed me a video of what he did that day. The two of them were in cahoots—Ryan had told his mom he wanted to stay home from school, play hooky, to help me. I had been stressed out about our pool, which had a leak in it. She let him.

Watching the video, I saw that my twelve-year-old son woke up minutes after I left for the city and spent all day drilling and hauling, doing grunt work. The name of the Bosch drill he used—Bulldog.

Once again, I was glad that Heather didn't listen to me. I certainly would have said no to staying home from school, but now I have no doubt that he learned more that day from manual labor than he would have learned from the greatest teachers. I know one thing he learned—he wants to earn enough one day to pay someone to fix the pool, unlike his dad who always tries to do it himself (thanks to Mr. E).

He showed tremendous strength of character and fitness in the game. And such humility—he didn't tell me what he did. He saved me a full day. Yes, sir—he's a bulldog, all right.

Heather and I always attended our boys' parent/teacher conferences. When Skyler was in the third grade, his teacher suggested that we should look at the class assignments which lined the hallway on our way out. At the beginning of the year, she had asked the students to write down their goals for that coming year. I thought, *This is my kind of teacher!*

As Heather and I read through a dozen or so in search of Skyler's, the theme was common.

I want to learn to read better.

I want to learn to write better.

I want to be better at arithmetic.

All worthy goals for a nine-year-old. Along with being proud, I'm sure many of those parents worked with their child at home in an attempt to reach those goals.

When Heather and I arrived at Skyler's, we were blown away. It was simple and to the point:

My goal for third grade is to help anyone who needs my help, because I believe I can help them.

I felt like we had just won the gold medal in the Parenting Olympics. My son's goals were probably the same ones Jesus had when he was nine. It doesn't get any better than that.

If my boys only take away one thing from me as a parent, I pray that they stick with their faith. I pray that they continue to lean on Jesus, keep him in their hearts, and lean on him through every failure and every victory.

Now that my sons are teenagers, it's our dogs who greet me at the door when I get home from work. Years earlier, one of my wise friends told me:

"There will be a time when they will rather be with their friends than with you."

We've arrived at those times.

I remembered Mr. Romano's words to me when I was a teenager:

"Show me your friends, and I'll show you who you are."

Our great founding father and first president, George Washington, at the amazing age of fourteen years, wrote his *Washington's Rules for Civility and Decent Behaviour in Company and Conversation.* In it, he states:

"Associate yourself with men of good quality, if you esteem your own reputation; for it is better to be alone than in bad company."

(Young ladies, the same holds true for you!)

We can't control the friends our children will choose forever. What we can do is try to help them form the character needed to choose friends wisely.

We feel very blessed to have both of our sons attend Delbarton School in Morristown, New Jersey. Heather and I were blown away on our very first visit. The students were engaging and intellectually curious, the faculty and staff were vibrant and dynamic. The school is ranked as the number one Catholic School in our state overall, and number two in the country. Delbarton has also been number one in the state for its athletics over the past two years, with a number of their sports teams winning a significant amount of league and state tournaments.

Delbarton is a place where boys become men. Our priest, Msgr. Geno, is an alumnus. Delbarton is directed by the Benedictine monks of St. Mary's Abbey—we fell in love with the school because of its values. The same values we teach our boys at home are reinforced at school, especially the following hallmarks:

Love of God and Neighbor, Prayer and Worship, Discipline, Humility, and Stewardship.

There is no perfect script for fatherhood. No "one size fits all" approach. We learn as we go, we make mistakes. While writing this book—in fact, while working on this particular chapter—a friend told me, "The best thing you can do as a parent is to shower your children with love."

I believe Heather and I have done this. At times, it's not easy to respond or react the way we should. Deep down at the core, our children want to know that we love them, that we care, that we value their place in the family.

I heard a group of teenagers talking about their curfews. One girl in particular didn't have one. The others envied her and complained about how strict their parents were, about having to be home earlier than the rest of the crowd.

"You're lucky. You get to come home whenever you want," they said.

"No, you're lucky," the girl responded. "Your parents love you!"

That same friend who told me about loving our kids also said this:

"The best gift you can give your sons is to love your wife."

Boy, do I. I still feel like I am on my honeymoon. Sure, Heather and I have our disagreements and arguments like every other couple. But our love is strong. Maybe we got lucky; maybe our different backgrounds, in their own way, solidified our belief in the importance of marriage. However it happened,

I'm thankful to God that I love Heather more today than yesterday. If that's even possible.

Sometimes I twirl Heather around in the aisle at the grocery store—I dance with her in the mall parking lot or in our kitchen while she's making dinner. Our boys watch, and when they both race to the car to open the door for their mother, I know that they're observing how I treat her. And trust me— when kids are watching, they are learning.

At our wedding reception, Heather's dad gave us some valuable advice, which he said his wife would want us to know:

Never go to bed angry.

In our twenty-plus years of marriage, we have lived that out. And our boys know it.

One of the visions I had of my future life, at the moment of the head-on collision, was of two young boys, smiling. And one of my favorite Christmas cards, which we sent to family and friends, is a picture of Ryan and Skyler playing in the grass, looking back at the camera and smiling. Those were the two boys in my vision.

I read once:

A man's wealth is not judged by his material possessions, but by the happiness of his family.

That makes me a very wealthy man.

I hope and pray that what Heather and I have taught our sons will be seeds that take root, grow strong, and produce great fruit in their lives. Here are some of the specific seeds we have planted in them over the years:

Believe in yourself.

Do your best.
Never give up.
Say "please" and "thank you."
Be honest.
Ask questions.
Read more.
Be kind.
Help others.
Laugh often.
Love lots.
Listen with your heart.
Cherish family and friends.
Live simply.
Be thankful.
Pray.

And, boys, I promise—I'll keep working on these myself.

CHAPTER ELEVEN

BE FAIR. PLAY HARD.

Do not neglect hospitality, for through it some have
unknowingly entertained angels (Hebrews 13:2).

A t the end of February 2000, I was still working for the gym on the Upper East Side, where my friend Joe had helped me get a job as a fitness trainer. I had moved up to a manager's position, responsible for the evening hours. The owners of the gym recognized my value—early on they had me working with all of their new clients because I had a one hundred percent conversion rate of keeping them coming back after their initial commitment. Not only that, but the evening hours were the busiest time at the gym, with clientele coming in from their high-paying Manhattan jobs to take advantage of the training I offered.

My pay structure as a manager was built around bonuses based on increased revenue. For the quarter that ended at the beginning of 2000, I had produced a 40 percent increase in revenue for the company. I showed up early, I worked late. The work ethic I had developed in baseball carried over to my job as a manager and fitness trainer.

When I got my bonus check for that quarter, however, it was based on a 25 percent increase in revenue—not the 40 percent I had produced for the business. When I questioned it, I was told that their bonus plan maxed out at 25 percent—there was nothing more they could do for me.

That planted a seed in my mind to start my own business. During the month of February, I contemplated starting a baseball camp. Spring was approaching, and I had contacts on the Upper East Side of New York City, while Randall's Island and Central Park offered fields where I could hold my camps.

While I entertained those thoughts, I could also hear my mom's sensible voice in the back of my mind:

You have a steady job.
You have health benefits.
You're getting a dependable check.
You're married now—you need to think about taking care
of your family.
Why would you risk all of that to start your own business?
What if it fails?

I think that last voice was my own, a holdover from my disappointment at getting cut by the Twins.

So, late in February on a cold afternoon—a typically overcast day in New York City at that time of year—I sat in my car on the Upper East Side. I was between 79th and 80th on Park Avenue, a couple of blocks away from the gym at the corner of 78th and Madison. I always drove into the city early to find a parking spot. While I sat there thinking about not being treated fairly by the gym owners, battling myself and my fear of stepping out on my own, an older gentleman got out of the car in front of me and walked back to my car. He was around sixty-five or seventy—he looked and was dressed like one of the retirees who frequent the sidewalks of that high-rent neighborhood.

I rolled my window down.

Now I know, in that moment, I showed hospitality to an angel.

"Why aren't you in baseball anymore?" he asked.

I guess it was shock. But for whatever reason, I didn't even think to ask him how he knew anything about me, especially that I had ever been involved in baseball. In this surreal moment in time, I reached into my pocket to get my wallet and pulled out my baseball card.

I handed it to him.

"See? I used to be a professional baseball player."

"I know. That's why I'm asking. Why aren't you still involved in baseball?"

I told him about the baseball camp I was thinking about starting. Finally, he said, "Well, you know what you need to do."

I'm not sure what happened next. I believe that I must have looked down to put my baseball card back in my wallet. Regardless, when I looked back up, he was gone.

It was time for me to head to the gym. I got out of my car and looked around. He wasn't back in his car. He wasn't walking down the street. I looked in every direction, but he had disappeared in the seconds it took me to look up and get out of my car.

Remember the scene in *Field of Dreams*, when the players from the past first come through the cornstalks onto the baseball field and then disappear back into the corn? I felt like that's what happened to me that cold February afternoon on the streets of New York City.

I wondered—

Was that guy really here?

However it happened, I believe that God sent one of his messengers, his guardian angels, to lead me out of the gym and into my own business.

I wanted to talk with him more, to ask questions. I felt like I had been in a trance while he stood outside my car. But as I walked the couple of blocks to work, I knew what I needed to do. I had to stop overthinking it, to quit planning and just do it—it was time to start my baseball business.

I had been talking myself out of doing it—I was letting fear lead. I believe that's what got me into trouble on the baseball field, when I started having self-doubts. But I wasn't going to let that stop me now. When Heather and I had dinner at Ossy's with her father, and he encouraged me to try it, I was even more convinced.

I don't have to worry about it, even if it fails.

I can always try something else.

It wasn't long until I realized that the owners of the gym had done me a favor. If I had remained satisfied with my job and situation there, I might not have had the urge and motivation to leave.

Within a day or so, I gave my two weeks' notice and began marketing my first baseball camp. I created brochures and business cards. I called my new enterprise "Every Boy's Dream." Around the same time, I started coaching sixth grade baseball three days a week at The Allen-Stevenson School, a private day school for boys on East 78th Street in Manhattan. Many of my first-year campers came from the school.

I worked with a few kids in the park, and before I knew it, I had more than a handful. My camp became a group lesson, which turned into a clinic. The boys were having so much fun, they didn't want to stop—the clinic became an after-school program in the fall and spring. After a couple of years, little brothers were old enough to join, and soon I had groups on every day of the week from different schools and at different ages.

No matter the kid's age or background, my philosophy always stayed the same. My program was value-based. Sure, I would love to see some of my kids become major leaguers. But my goal was to help form quality human beings, whatever their playing capability might be.

I always taught the proper fundamentals of the game—how to run, throw, and hit. But as I drilled those basic baseball skills, I instilled in them good sportsmanship, respect, teamwork, and hustle. Without being preachy, I tried to teach them by example and, with my words, the Golden Rule:

Do unto others as you would want done to you.

Overcoming fears and obstacles, the importance of preparation and persistence, and good old-fashioned grit—these were the values I held up for every boy who passed through one of my camps, teams, clinics, and after-school programs. There was always a lesson to be learned. I saw my boys work together as a team, and I saw them leave with smiles on their faces.

One day, at the end of one of my sessions, a gentleman came up to thank me for a great practice.

"Who's your son?" I asked.

"Oh, my son's not in the program. I was just on my way home from work and stopped to watch your practice."

He went on to tell me that it brought back negative memories of when he was a young boy.

"I never remember Little League being that much fun," he said. "When I watched your team, I couldn't help but think of my son, who has been asking for a baseball glove. I have been avoiding it because I didn't want him to have the same experience I had as a young boy. I've been trying to protect him from the anxiety I had when I played."

"It's not too late," I said. "The Modell's on 86th Street is still open."

I smiled as I watched this gentleman run through Central Park in his three-piece suit.

The first day of practice at The Allen-Stevenson School was in the gym. I met a young fellow who said he had decided to play lacrosse instead of baseball. This eleven-year-old was quick with his words—sharp, witty, and wise beyond his years. I asked him why he didn't want to play baseball.

"Baseball isn't fun," he said.

I wasn't going to let that go as a final answer. I prodded him with a few questions, and he altered his response a bit.

"I didn't have fun when I played it last year."

I knew I could work with that. Obviously, if any kid enjoys something else more, he or she should go for it. And let's be honest—baseball can be boring, especially at the fifth and sixth grade level. A few more questions, and I found out why he didn't have fun.

"They always put me in right field, and I always batted last."

This interaction with a wise and honest eleven-year-old became the foundation of my long and successful second baseball career.

I formed much of my coaching philosophy that day. I decided that the game really needed two different approaches at the youth level. For my more competitive travel teams, which used only the best players, I could demand more and put them where they could perform at the top of their game. They were ready to learn what it was like at the high school, college, and even professional level of play. Only the best pitchers pitch. The best batters land in the front of the lineup. You play to win, and they need to understand that.

But at the lower school and recreational level, I needed to take a very different approach. What happened forty years earlier to the gentleman I met in the park, and had just happened to this great kid, should never happen. This was something I could easily change.

First, I understood that as a coach for those young people there is more at stake than wins and losses. Don't misunderstand me—show me someone who likes to lose, and I'll show you a loser. But when I focus on the players themselves, and whether or not they're having fun *playing the game*, I have my priorities straight at that level of competition.

During my first assignment, my first goal as a youth baseball coach was to make sure that every kid felt like he belonged, regardless of how proficient he was at the game. My approach, which was different from everyone I ever played against, was to make sure that each boy got a chance to hit first. They each got to pitch. No one got stuck on the bench, or in right field, or batting last.

Of course, I tell them and show them how to play the game, and I encourage them to try harder and not give up. I helped them set achievable goals that were just out of reach. Like the ones Ryan and Skyler had when we played one-on-one basketball—have a plan to score just one more basket each time we match up.

When I look back at the many lessons I've learned from baseball, I realize how much the game has added to my life— setting goals, designing strategies to improve skills, sacrificing myself for the sake of the team; these are principles that helped me in the classroom, in the workplace, in my relationships, and in my community. I wanted to pass that along to the kids I coached.

When I played catch with my boys, I made them chase the ball if they overthrew me. I started this with the players I coached, and eventually their throws became more accurate. I had the entire group working as a unit. They would cover for the weakest link, and if they didn't, I reminded them.

I rewarded those who encouraged, who helped, who demonstrated kindness and humility. It didn't take long for the group to start competing to exhibit those qualities. *Praise*— we all want it, we all need it, and children bloom like spring flowers when they receive it. I knew I couldn't make a kid love baseball—but there were things that I could control, and which could make the game fun for everyone who wanted to try. Just show up and try.

Early in that first year at the school, I asked the boys to hustle from the locker room one day—my plan was to take our bus from the Upper East Side over to Randall's Island and give them some batting practice before our game. When none of them arrived by my proposed deadline for leaving, I decided to write out my line-up card based on the order they showed up at the bus.

As they meandered out to join me, I made sure they entered the bus one at a time so that I could get my batting order right. I had eleven players on that roster. It just so happened that numbers ten and eleven onto the bus that day were the team's best players. Both were pitchers, and both would have helped us somewhere in the middle of the line-up.

I wanted to teach them to hustle, to listen to the person in charge, and to understand that no one on the team received preferential treatment because they happened to have more baseball skills than anyone else.

And here's another lesson from that day.

Just as the game started, I could hear rumbling from the parents behind our dugout.

"Who the heck is this new coach?"

"He doesn't know anything about baseball."

"How did he get hired in the first place?"

"Why isn't my son playing? He's the best on the team!"

Standing in the coach's box by third base, I thought, *Oh boy, I guess I have stirred it up.*

When the son of the man who made that last statement finally got up to bat, he scorched one down the left field line. Actually, that's not quite right—there was no line. I wasn't sure if it had worn away with time, or if they didn't use chalk on Randall's Island. But for whatever reason, there was no line, and the ump called it a foul ball.

The dad went bonkers on the umpire, and then he came after me.

"Why don't you argue that call? What kind of coach are you?"

My plan was to wait until the end of the game to address any concerns the parents might have. But I needed to handle that situation then and there. I left the third base coaching box and went to the fence to talk with him.

"The umpire is seventeen years old. He's out here, doing this, to earn a few bucks. Yes, I had a better view than most, standing in the third base box. Your son's hit may very well have been fair. But that call that the ump made—it does not take away from your son's great swing and great hit."

I was trying to use every psychology tool in my kit, not only to diffuse the tension but to teach a lesson.

"I teach your son, and every member of this team, not to argue calls. What kind of example would I set if I didn't practice that as well? Umpires make judgment calls—fair or foul, safe or out, ball or strike. I will never argue a judgment call. Not ever. Now, if an umpire gets a rule wrong, I will gladly point that out, in a nice way, so that he doesn't get it wrong the next time."

I was on a roll.

"This is sixth grade baseball. Now let me tell you the kind of coach I am."

I told him my philosophy for drawing up a line-up, and how players would move around the diamond and within the batting order on a regular basis.

"But for today's line-up," I continued, "I made it based on the lack of hustle the team showed in the locker room before we even got on the bus to come to the game."

I didn't know how he would respond, and frankly, it didn't matter. I had made my decision as to how I would coach and handle my team, because it was what I believed in. I know that there have been, and always will be, people who don't agree.

I didn't have to wait long for this father's reply.

"I'm sorry, Coach. You are right," he said. "Thank you for teaching my son this important lesson."

I lived to coach another day.

Back in New Jersey, my sons started playing t-ball at around four or five. My initial plan was to only coach them in the backyard and to sit in the bleachers with Heather for their games. That plan didn't last long.

For Ryan's first game, he was playing third base. Ryan bats right-handed, but he throws left-handed. It's rare for a lefty to play anywhere but first base, outfield, or on the pitcher's mound. At four or five, however, I had no problem with him playing third. I knew it wouldn't be long until he was locked into one of those other positions on the field.

With the runners on first and second, Ryan fielded a grounder, moved over two feet to step on third, and then fired one to first base. The ball whizzed past the first baseman, who was doing what most five-year-olds do on a baseball field—staring aimlessly into the sky, his glove on the ground, kicking up a pile of dirt.

The coach then told Ryan that he shouldn't have stepped on third.

"Next time, just throw to first base."

That was the moment when I officially stepped in to coach my boys in an organized way.

Years later, Ryan was pitching in a travel game. He was ten years old. The other team's coach was a big burly guy, about 240 pounds. During several pitches he said to his batter, "Here comes the meatball."

Each time he said it, I could tell that Ryan got distracted. Unless they're words of praise and encouragement, I don't believe it's ever appropriate for a coach to direct any comments towards their opponent's team members, especially derogatory comments aimed at young kids!

Ryan somehow managed to strike the batter out with his "meatball." I called the coach over before the next inning started. In my third base coaching box, separated by a strong fence, I felt safe—along with the fact that my first base coach, Police Lieutenant Mason Maher, is about the same size as the guy.

"Hey, coach, I know you probably didn't mean it the wrong way, but I'm not sure using 'meatball' to describe my pitcher's pitch is the right adjective to use when you're coaching your batter."

His curly red hair, popping out of the side and back of his hat, matched the complexion of his face. Along with his 240 pounds, he stood around six foot four, with legs like tree trunks coming out of his shorts (which might have been a little too short). I really didn't know what to expect.

"Ya' know—meatball, good pitch," he explained.

I had heard him speak to his team, not only during that game but in previous ones as well. His tone was harsh. He yelled and screamed when mistakes were made. I saw the look of fear on his team—pressing, trying harder not to mess up than to do well. They didn't want to be called out, embarrassed, or humiliated in front of their teammates, their opponents, their parents, the fans.

I said nothing about those things. But this opportunity gave me a small window to address what he was saying to his batter indirectly about my pitcher's fastball. I quickly got in one more important line.

"These boys are ten years old, and they take in every word you say. Forget I ever said anything. I know you didn't mean anything by it."

And I went back to the coaching box, keeping one eye on the big guy. I knew enough from the old saying—*Praise in public, criticize in private*—to hope I hadn't crossed a line.

If I had yelled back at him as he screamed "meatball," I would not have accomplished anything. At least nothing good. I might have antagonized him and made the situation worse.

He calmed down that inning, and when the third out was made, he ran me down before I got to the safe zone behind my fence. He reached out his hand.

"I never looked at it like that before. I know I am hard on these kids. No one ever called me out on it. I've said a lot worse things to these guys than 'hit the meatball.' Thank you."

I shook the man's hand.

Before that season ended, he came up to Ryan and spoke.

"Your dad made me a better coach, and I now have a better relationship with my son. I was always hardest on him."

We don't always know the impact we are having on others. What I do know is that there is a ripple effect that takes place. We can do good, or we can do harm.

I know I am blessed. These are two situations in which I spoke up at the right time, and now I have important stories to share. My prayer is that they can help others.

Some people get it. Some people eventually get it. Other people will never get it.

I remember sitting in the stands watching a Little League game. The two coaches were battling it out, trying to outsmart one another, trying to be like major league skippers.

In the bottom of the last inning, the team's best hitter stepped up to the plate. The bases were loaded with two outs, and the team batting was down by five runs. A grand slam would put them within one run. The coach for the team in the field tells his pitcher to intentionally walk the batter. I know many people would say that was a smart decision. In a scenario in which winning is the primary goal, I would agree. But in this situation, I would have handled it very differently.

Let the kids play.

Who knows—what if the pitcher strikes him out and now has a proud story to tell? What if the batter hits one to the warning track, and the outfielder makes a great play to save the game? What if the batter does hit a grand slam? The next batter could make the last out, and the team in the field would still win.

Youth coaches:

It's not about you!

Let the kids play. Let umps umpire.
And parents:

Please just watch the game!

Here's what that kid heard his coach tell him:

I don't believe that you can get this batter out.

It's hard for kids to learn to believe in themselves if they know that their mentors, their coaches, don't believe in them to begin with.

In seven years of coaching recreational league baseball, my teams had a record of eighty-five wins and five losses, with five league championships and three undefeated seasons. While that is pretty impressive by any standard, the record I am most proud of is the return rate of my players—98 percent. These children likely will not move on to play professionally. In fact, most of them may never even play high school ball. What I do see is that all of them improve, and they all leave the field with smiles on their faces.

I had the opportunity to meet with and share my coaching philosophy with a Major League Baseball executive in the commissioner's office. For some time, the experts have bemoaned the fact that fewer and fewer kids are playing baseball, especially in urban and low-income environments. I feel like my approach could help turn that tide.

I would love for all little league and youth programs to apply my method of fairness, one that gives every child a chance to contribute. This enjoyable, rewarding experience will ensure that they have positive childhood memories. These boys will one day pass their love of baseball down through generations, becoming lifelong fans.

At the end of one of our undefeated regular seasons, a parent came up to me and asked for guidance. We were in the third round of the playoffs, and she said her son had a conflict for our next game. My personal opinion has always been that God, family, and school should come before your sports commitment. If it were a communion or bar mitzvah, a family birthday, or an important test to study for—I had no problem with a kid missing our game.

She then told me—his conflict was a scheduled photo session for a band that he played in.

"What does your son want to do?" I asked.

She hadn't asked him.

"Well, I think he should be here with his teammates. They can use photoshop to get him in the band picture."

She finally asked her son, a thought she hadn't considered before. He smiled. He was happy to be asked, and he gave a big yes to being at our game.

Now for a bit of background.

This kid hadn't gotten one hit all season long. He may have made contact with the ball once or twice, but his season consisted of mostly strikeouts and a few walks. I think it's safe to say that many coaches would love to have one of their bottom tier players miss an important game. One less out, one less potential screw up.

For me, however, I saw that I had a young boy who wanted to be with his teammates. And who knows, maybe something special would happen!

During the game, in the bottom of the sixth with our team down by a run, this young man ripped into a ball. He went "shopping in the gap"—he lined a double to left center to tie the game.

I will never forget the smile on that kid's face when he got to second. I glanced over at his mom, who was beaming. Unfortunately, we went on to lose the game that day. But something much bigger than what the scoreboard showed took place. I pray that the relationship between that mother and son grew a bit stronger, and that she asked for his input more often. That young man now has a story to share with his children. He didn't quit, he didn't give up, and he kept swinging. For that one moment, I don't doubt that he felt like a major leaguer.

Be Fair. Play Hard.

It's the motto I use for all of my coaching work. It's the advice I give to every ballplayer, young or old. I believe that this advice sends a bigger message:

Character, above winning, is what counts most.

One night in 2006, I was telling my boys a bedtime story about a player who was having difficulty being a good sport. He threw his equipment. He wouldn't listen to instructions. He was disrespectful to everyone. He wasn't inclusive. Just as my biological father served as an example of how not to be a dad, this kid was an example of how not to be sportsmanlike. He wouldn't hustle. He had no concept of what it meant to be a part of a team—or if he did, he didn't show it.

My boys wanted to hear all about this kid. But they especially wanted to know how Coach Dan handled it.

This was at the very beginning of my coaching career. For the boys who really wanted to play and learn, discipline came easy. You sit them down. You take away something that means a lot to them, to show them that there are consequences for bad behavior. But what do you do with a kid who doesn't care? My normal methods of discipline would only escalate his bad behavior.

I pulled him aside and made him my captain.

"I need you to let me know if any of your teammates aren't being a good sport."

He took his responsibility to heart, and I had little trouble with him after that.

Sportsmanship is something that has become a lost art in much of American sports. It means playing the game the fair and honest way. It means being respectful of teammates and coaches. Good sports listen, they are patient while waiting their turn, and they have compassion for their opponents. They include their teammates, they share, they are humble after a win, and they keep their heads held high after a loss. A good sport doesn't argue a call or throw his or her equipment.

Go to any athletic field, in any town, on any given weekend, and you will experience some form of unsportsmanlike conduct. Unfortunately, a lot of this inappropriate behavior comes from adults. While I believe that most parents and coaches start off with good intentions, somewhere along the way they get caught up in the moment. In their effort to create winners, they forget about the ethics of the game. We need to set a better example.

Basically, good sportsmanship means good manners. I think most people would agree that this is something we could use more of in our culture.

During a family gathering, I had a dozen children at full attention while telling them Coach Dan stories. At that moment, I knew I had something special. I shared that experience with a dear friend, Pat Tomkins, who suggested I write a children's book. The seed was planted. I dedicated the book to Pat, who passed away before it was published. Her relentless pursuit of teaching good manners continues to inspire me.

In 2006, I shopped the manuscript around to many publishers, only to receive a pile of rejection letters. I put it on the shelf for six years, and then I decided to take action. I hired an illustrator, had the book printed, and published it myself because of the importance of the message. *Coach Dan on Sportsmanship* got some national exposure. I hope this part of the "Coach Dan" story inspires others to keep plugging away at their dreams. I am grateful the media recognized the importance of my message.

Book signings, school book fairs, and visits to speak at elementary schools became quite common. It then led to TV and radio appearances, which led to being called on as an expert in the field of youth and professional sports. I was asked to comment on current events, like the controversy over steroid users getting into the Baseball Hall of Fame, or how the cheating scandal in the MLB affects our children. This led to meetings with Nike, Sesame Street, and Major League Baseball.

But, once again, God had other plans in store for me.

CHAPTER TWELVE

SHAPING LIVES

On the Ides of March 2000, I left the gym and became an entrepreneur. One of my older clients at the gym told me that she did not want to train with anyone else. While I planned and started my first baseball camp, I agreed to train her in her home.

When that first camp ended, the mom of one of my campers asked me to train her. While going in and out of her building on the Upper East Side, I met more people who became my training clients. Word of mouth spread, and my new business grew. Carrying over from my time at the gym, I bind myself to my trainer-confidentiality clause, which I take very seriously. I have not, and will not, ever reveal the names of my clients.

While working at the gym, I found out how much I love helping others reach their goals. Of course, to receive my accreditation as a fitness trainer, I learned about all the muscles in the body, along with their Latin names; but my knowledge of human anatomy wasn't what attracted my clients. They wanted me to keep it simple and motivate them to do more than they would if left on their own, while keeping it safe so they didn't get injured. Sure, it was crucial that I teach them the correct form as they got started, but it was the motivation to keep going, even when they didn't want to or feel like it, which was even more important.

As I experienced in my own training to become a professional athlete, consistency is key. "Repetition is the mother of skill"—an adage that has proven true over and over in my life and in the lives of my clients. With diligence and time, I have literally watched people's bodies transform in front of my eyes.

One of my first clients as a trainer on my own was a young boy, around nine years old. I'm still working with that young man today—he just celebrated his twenty-sixth birthday. What started as exercise training moved into sports training and then life coaching. Throughout, my job was to encourage, to motivate, to plant seeds. He had the personal commitment to apply what I gave him, the fortitude to overcome tough hurdles, and the strong mindset that I found in so many of my successful Upper East Side clients.

Of course, I wasn't 100 percent successful with everyone. One woman, with whom I had been working for several months, complained that she wasn't losing any weight. I asked about her diet.

"Cottage cheese, salads, and grilled lean meats."

Within days of that conversation, I was walking down Madison Avenue to meet with another client when I saw her through the window of a diner. I briefly watched her dig into a mound of french fries and then take a large bite of a double cheeseburger. I didn't tell her what I saw, but her actions told me much more than her answers to my questions. A person must be open to changing their lifestyle, their mindset, their belief system. To have the will for something to happen is important. But that's merely the starting point. Taking the actions necessary to put that will into motion is essential.

I have learned as much or more from my clients as they have learned from me. Many of them have become lifelong friends. A few have mentored me along the way, and I have been able to pass their lessons along to the next generation.

One older gentleman comes from a much different spiritual place and experience than me. Over our years together, we have had many fascinating and challenging discussions with each other during his training sessions. I have told him how much I appreciate our time together—we have sharpened each other's reasoning along the way.

One family I've been working with, basically since the beginning of my business, has been a particular inspiration to me. I watched the parents interact with their children—strict and steadfast on one hand, and yet loving and grace-filled on the other. I learned that, as parents, it isn't our job to be friends with our children. That may come later, when they are adults. But our job when they're young is to train them in the way they should go (Proverbs 22:6).

Every member of that family has a warm and gentle soul. And they have proven to be incredibly generous. I have found that to be true of many of my clients—they are generous with their time, with their talent, and with their treasure. I work hard at putting that into practice in my own life, as an example for my family and my life coaching clients.

In 2012, I received a letter for Christmas. It read:

We have a holiday tradition of designating one individual we know as the recipient of a very special, one-time secret Santa gift.

You and your family are receiving this gift this year. We so admire how honest and hardworking you are and how very much you care for your family. Your values are so incredibly right in a world that often doesn't reward doing the right thing.

We know that you have made some decisions about the hours you work in order to spend more time with your boys. "Lucky boys," is what we have to say about that. We also know that this would be easier to do if you were not concerned about future education expenses—potentially high school and definitely college.

So here is a small contribution to an existing or new education savings account for each boy. With the miracle of compound interest, this will be worth more when the boys need it for their educations.

We hope that our gift to you all is the gift of more time together.

This extremely generous gift showed me that Santa doesn't always come in a red suit. By sharing this letter, I hope it will inspire you—as it has Heather and me—to pay it forward, no matter how small. This gesture of anonymous giving also proved to me that I was on the right track.

Hard work, strong character, and solid family values do get rewarded.

As I've mentioned, my fitness training soon began to include life coaching. My gift for reading people, for understanding what drives and motivates them, translated well into this new service I could offer my clients.

I take very seriously the opportunity I have to help shape someone's life or business. I work with kids, adults, and corporations. By addressing in my own life a lack of mental focus, which possibly prevented me from achieving my boyhood dream of playing in the big leagues, I'm now able to train others in applying techniques to reach their specific goals.

While I've had the fitness part of my life on track since I was very young, focus is now a driving force behind my work, my relationship with my wife, and my parenting. I know what worked for me in my quest to achieve the improbable, and I also know what did not.

I continue to learn from others. Motivational speakers have always intrigued me—self-help gurus like Napoleon Hill, Zig Ziglar, and Anthony Robbins. I read their books, I listen to them speak, and I've learned that if I don't apply what I hear in my life and my relationships, then it has accomplished nothing. By putting into practice their motivational techniques, these men helped me make the leap from steady job to sole proprietor, have stronger relationships with my family and friends, and readjust and realign my goals.

We all need our coaches! I think back over the coaches I've had, the people who helped shape and form me. And I'm not just referring to my baseball coaches, though a number of them have been extremely important in my life. It's everyone from my forever hero—my mom—to my father-in-law, to many of my clients as well.

My motivational speaker coaches have taught me that focus is power. We all know people who are Chicken Little-like, or like the character from "Saturday Night Live," Debbie Downer—complainers, always seeing the worst in situations and in others.

This can be fixed with focus—the things you choose to concentrate on with your mind. It isn't wishful thinking; it is setting your mind to take action toward your goals. It's one little step at a time. Small steps build momentum.

Have you seen Bill Murray's movie, *What about Bob?* It's hilarious. But the principle offered by the psychiatrist character, played by Richard Dreyfuss, works.

Baby steps, Bob.

That's what I'm talking about.

Baby steps.

If you change your belief system, start doing rather than hoping, you will find yourself with small successes that eventually lead to big change.

Here's an idea—don't eat that doughnut for breakfast. That's a small step, but by year's end, you will feel healthier and likely lighter. Once you take those steps, you're motivated to stop the fast food and cut down the alcohol intake—maybe even cut it out altogether.

You've probably heard this all of your life:

Everything in moderation.

Yes, I will occasionally eat fast food, and I do like my every-now-and-then doughnut, but I consciously choose not to make either part of my daily or even weekly routine.

Focus is all about training our minds. Read as much as you can. Never stop learning. Albert Einstein once said, "Education commences at birth and ends at death."

As kids, we were always trying to get better at things. Perfecting a craft, playing an instrument, running faster, jumping higher, improving at a sport. Why don't we take the same approach when it comes to learning as adults?

Training our minds, like training our bodies, is a lot simpler than we think. In fact, life is simpler than we think. The recent pandemic and quarantine forced us all to slow things down. Yes, it's been hard, and, for many, financially debilitating. But with the negative comes the opportunity—more time with family, more time in prayer, more time to be appreciative of the little things. Have you slowed down recently to enjoy a cool breeze, a sunset, or the reflection of trees bouncing off a body of water?

Do something every day. Remember:

Repetition is the mother of skill.

But you must repeat the right things! If you have that doughnut or bagel every day, they will add up by the end of the year. Over time, your metabolism doesn't work as efficiently. The same workout that kept the bagel off your hips in the past no longer works.

I call it a lifestyle change when my clients join the wonderful world of fitness and focus. As I said, it can be simple:

Move more. Eat right.

I tailor my workouts for each client. There's no one-size-fits-all in fitness training or in life coaching. If the session is too hard, the client may not return. If it's too easy, they will not see results. Slowly, step by step, we increase the intensity and duration of the exercise.

And let me say this again:

Do something every day.

In addition to weight training, which is necessary for bone density, we need cardio for our hearts, stretching for our elasticity, and balance for our well-being. When you're done with this chapter, go do something active to reach one of your goals.

I've learned, in my own life and from my clients, that *attitude* is crucial for both fitness and focus.

Smiles are contagious. Mother Teresa said, "Greet each person with a smile, for the smile is the beginning of love."

My family and I live in New Jersey, but I still work in New York City. I drive in, park my car, and then ride my bike from appointment to appointment. One of my favorite things to do while biking is to try and get people to smile. And I don't just mean the people I work with. That has always been a priority in my work, and I make sure it happens, even in the middle of a workout. I'm talking about strangers that I pass—the crossing guard on the street, the elderly person sitting on the park bench. Most people these days walk with their heads down, buried in their phones, unable to see the beautiful bird that flies over. They miss the smile of a child holding hands with his father while trying to keep the ice cream from dripping all the way down to the bottom of the cone.

Life is full of these little moments; moments that can bring joy to us and to others, if we bring the right attitude and focus, paying attention to see them when they happen.

I remind people as I pass them to look up from their phones, to smile, to take a deep breath. Stop and look at the flowerbed. See the beauty in every passerby. My typical goal is to get twenty people to smile each day.

I get strange responses at times—some people think I'm crazy. I usually start with conversation. If that fails, I go to, "How about just one smile?"

This simple question works almost every time. If I have to ask twice, my conversion rate is 100 percent.

The wisest man who ever lived said this:

Ask, and you shall receive.

I don't know what's going on in their lives—maybe heartache and pain are consuming them that day. But when I see their faces light up, I feel the Lord smile down on me. I'm not looking for anything in return except a smile! As we share that most beautiful of facial expressions, I believe that we also share a feel-good moment. Maybe, because of a smile, that person will be nicer to their children, or spouse, or employee, or boss.

Maybe that simple gesture changes more than the course of their day. I may be idealistic, but can we imagine what our world would be like if more people were laughing? If more of us encouraged laughter? I suspect the world would be much more pleasant if this was the case.

I'm offering you a challenge. Make today mean something. Get twenty people to smile today. Or, start with a baby step— get five people to smile today! See if you also feel your Heavenly Father smiling down on you.

As I travel between my clients on the streets of New York City, there are two people I have connected with that I want to tell you about—Dimitri and Irene.

Dimitri is a hot dog vendor who sets up shop on the northwest corner of Madison Avenue and 71st Street. He's been selling "dirty water dogs" for forty years (that's a hot dog seasoned in a vat of hot water with onion, vinegar, red pepper, cumin, and nutmeg). I must confess that I've had my fair share of them, often because I'm in a hurry to get to my next client, but mainly because I like to visit my friend.

He's around sixty-five years old, I think, but the outdoor work has aged him. He's out there in rain, heat, ice, and snow. He works for someone else and takes home one third of what he earns on a given day. A third goes toward the cost of goods, and the other third goes to the owner, who has dozens of these carts throughout the city.

I tried to talk Dimitri into being his own boss, but he's happier not being an owner. He gets picked up by the truck at 5:00 p.m., tosses his stand in the back, and is driven to his studio apartment in Queens.

I am drawn to this man for many reasons. He smiles. He works hard every day and doesn't complain. He hopes to go back to his homeland of Greece in a year or two—he wants Heather and me to visit him there. I stop on my bike, exchange a smile, buy something that I really don't need or want. But he and I connect as fellow travelers in this life.

Then there is Irene. A homeless woman, she sits in Central Park with her two bags. I've joined her for lunch more times than I can count. We talk. She prefers the street over the shelter. I can tell that she suffers from mental illness—sometimes she is disconnected. I know when I can stop and when I should keep moving, but I never pass without calling her name and giving her a smile.

On the surface, Dimitri and Irene are very different from the clients I work with on New York's Upper East Side. But by stopping to spend time with them, to listen and to care about them and their lives, I have found things that we all, as human beings created by God to love and to be loved, have in common.

Over the past twenty years I've had the opportunity to work with individuals who are in the big leagues of their respective professions—politicians from Washington, DC; Hollywood movie stars; professional athletes; doctors; lawyers; investment bankers; business executives. My clients come from every religion and from no religion. They're gay and straight. They're Black, White, Hispanic, and Asian. They're liberal, conservative, Republican, Democrat, and Independent. In the process of working with such a diverse group of wonderful people, I've become more than just a trainer and life coach—sometimes I'm a "therapist."

Not only do I need to be a good listener, I also need to ask the right questions. My on-the-job training has taught me that I do not necessarily need to give the "correct" answer—I seek to lead my clients to discover for themselves what their solution is.

As a fitness trainer and life coach, not only have I doubled as a therapist, I've also served as an interior designer, a travel agent, a swim instructor, a tutor, a mentor, a consultant, a confidante, and always a friend. I've had the opportunity to help many individuals and businesses reach their full potential.

I cannot stress enough the importance of the mind and the role it plays in surviving, in winning, in reaching our goals. For all of us, failure is imminent. While my fitness was never in question, I didn't have the mental toughness, focus, and attitude I needed to succeed in professional baseball that one bad year with the Twins.

Think about it—for every professional baseball player who makes it to the Hall of Fame (other than pitchers), they failed seven out of ten times as a hitter at the plate!

That requires resilience. We must put behind us that last failure and attack the next problem with confidence and determination. To succeed at anything, we must be able to bounce back from failure.

Here is my list of qualities that I seek to instill in every one of my clients:

Focus
Attitude
Resiliency
Visualization
Concentration
Goal Setting

I believe that each and every one of us has three dimensions—we are a spirit, we have a mind, and we live in a body. When we're right with God, when we allow His Spirit to consume us, we are able to get our minds and our souls right. Saint Paul tells us that our bodies are the temple of the Holy Spirit (1 Corinthians 6:19). To honor God, we also want to keep our bodies in shape, the bodies He has placed us in. Also, we never know when we may need to lean on them!

I needed all three of my own dimensions to seek total wellness during those days I had to combat and beat COVID-19.

CHAPTER THIRTEEN

NEWFOUND FAITH

I was on my way to an 8 a.m. training session on the Upper West Side of Manhattan, early on a Saturday morning. It must have been around 7:15 a.m. when I got on Route 4, heading east from my home. As was my custom, I was talking with God as I drove. But this conversation was more serious than most. I was at a crossroad, and I needed to make a decision.

"God, I can't do this alone."

That's all I remember saying. Then the floodgates opened. I broke down, sobbing like a baby. I had to pull over to get myself together. It lasted for twenty or thirty minutes—I received another Holy Spirit infusion, similar to what I experienced that night in our apartment when I first forgave my father. Tears, chills, and then I was filled with God's love—it was overpowering.

Once I was able to drive again, I pulled into my usual place to get gas. But the only thing usual about this experience was the place and the man who worked there. I had seen him before—he spoke with an accent that made me think he was from somewhere in the Caribbean. Before that morning, "hello," "how's it going," and "goodbye" was about the extent of our communication.

This day, however, words began to gush out of me.

"God bless you! Thank you for all that you do. I know this can be a thankless job. But I want you to know that you're appreciated, that God is good, and that our very good God loves you!"

I had never seen him smile so big.

Because of my schedule that day, I parked on the Upper East Side and ran through Central Park for my first appointment. As I was running, a woman jogged beside me for a short distance. I couldn't help myself—

"You're doing great! Keep it up—you can do this!"

Words of encouragement for this stranger again poured out of me, and I was again repaid with a huge smile.

Once I left the park, I poked my head into a butcher shop where I occasionally stop to get some cuts to take home. The guys waved, had big smiles on their faces, and I yelled out, "God bless you! Have a great day!"

Next stop: a convenience store where I often got a breakfast smoothie. The same guy I normally saw was at the counter. He was from somewhere in the Middle East—I had always assumed he was Muslim.

"You know, God loves you!" I said.

Another big smile and lots of nods of his head.

When I went to the smoothie station, right by the sign that offered either the strawberry-banana-kiwi or apple-ginger flavors, there was a picture of Jesus. I had never seen it there before.

My client lived nearby in a building on Broadway. By the door, in his usual spot, was a homeless guy, clearly Asian, with ten or twelve bags around him. Without thinking, I said to him, "What are you doing here? You know what you need to do. God has a plan for you."

It was much later when I realized I had used the same words that God's messenger had said to me the day I decided to start my own business.

I never saw that man again.

As I went into the building I was greeted by the doorman. He and I had conversations before, but never about faith.

"Whatever you're going through," I said, "God wants you to know He's got it. He's with you."

Tears welled up in his eyes. He told me he was going through a difficult time with his wife and kids and asked me to pray for him.

What happened in my car that morning? What had changed in me?

I can only describe it as a fresh anointing of God's Holy Spirit. After that experience, I could no longer keep it to myself. It was overflowing, spilling out of me—living water that I couldn't contain. I had to share it with others.

Whoever believes in me, as scripture says: Rivers of living water will flow from within him (John 7:38).

I was that person! I left my home that morning as a person of quiet, intimate faith in my God. But with that experience on Route 4, I was transformed into one of God's messengers.

Another time I was on my way to a field in Central Park for one of my Friday afternoon programs with my baseball bag slung over my shoulder. My mind was focused—I knew I was looking at four or five hours in the park before heading home.

It had been raining that day, and there were puddles everywhere. I entered the park on 79th Street, on the south side of the Metropolitan Museum of Art. As I went under an overpass, I saw an older man sitting on a bench, bags surrounding him. He was wringing water from his soaking wet socks.

I stopped. I had never seen this man, probably in his fifties, in the park before. But something made me stop. I sat down beside him. He didn't ask for anything—he did look at me, but his eyes were vacant, like he was looking straight through me. I had no idea what he was thinking. So many homeless people in the city suffer from mental illness.

I watched him continue to try to wring out his wet socks. I didn't even think about it—I took off my shoes and socks and handed the latter to him.

Then, when he looked at me, his eyes were completely different. They sparkled and shone in multiple colors, like a rainbow. Still, he said nothing. He simply took the socks.

I had never done anything like that before. And I haven't since. But I can't fully describe the joy, the contentment, and satisfaction I felt as I continued on my way to the field. There was no audible voice from Heaven speaking to me. And yet, I "heard" my Heavenly Father say:

With you, my son, I am well pleased.

I felt God's pleasure. It's a feeling I'll never forget.

That simple act of taking off my socks and handing them to that man may well have been the single most important—the best thing—I have ever done in my life.

For the next four hours, I wore my baseball turf shoes with no socks. With every step I took, I was reminded of how that man lived, every moment of every day. The blisters I developed continued to remind me for a number of days that he needed those socks more than anything else I could have offered him.

I tell you that story, not to say:

Hey, look at me.

It is a testimony of how we can be led by God. My Father put me in that place, on that day, to see that man, and He gave me the grace to respond with love, compassion, and mercy. Life doesn't get much better than that.

If only I were always that in tune with what the Father is saying to me.

I mentioned earlier that I had the opportunity to meet with Major League Baseball to discuss my philosophy for coaching Little League and encouraging a love of the game in young players. It wasn't so easy getting that meeting. And I may have missed a "God moment" in my life by placing too much importance on it.

I sent out multiple emails and did everything I could think of to get a face-to-face with the head of Major League Baseball. Finally, I get a voicemail from one of the executives in the League office, telling me that the new commissioner had passed my information along to him and that we should set up a meeting. I cannot tell you how excited I was—I thought it was the opportunity of a lifetime.

I knew that my coaching strategies could make a huge difference for Little Leaguers. I had seen it work. My results were impressive—not only my winning percentage, but the return rate of my players from year-to-year.

I was on the Upper East Side for a training session with one of my clients the afternoon of my scheduled meeting. I finished my session, changed into my best suit, and, with an hour to spare before the meeting, I decided to go into a church and pray. At the corner of Lexington Avenue and 76th is a beautiful church, St. Jean Baptiste. The doors were open. I went in and quietly made my way into a pew and kneeled down.

At that point in my life, I rarely, if ever, prayed for myself. I was more than willing to pray for others, but I didn't want God to think that I was too caught up in my own wants. But on this day, I prayed for His leading, for Him to give me the right words to say, that I could effect change for the better, for Little League baseball players and for the game I have loved all my life. I must say, I wouldn't have minded if a position working for Major League Baseball came out of it either.

I figured there was more than one way to make it to the major leagues!

Just as I started my prayers, a woman came up from behind and tapped me on the shoulder. I was surprised—there were only three or four of us spread around the church that afternoon, and I had picked a spot away from the others. I turned around and looked at her. She had red hair, and she was wearing a white dress with polka dots on it.

"You know, Pope Francis is in town and celebrating mass at St. Patrick's tonight. I have an extra ticket to see him this afternoon," she said. "Would you like it?"

"What time?"

Those were the first words out of my mouth.

"Four o'clock."

Which was the exact time of my meeting. I felt a bit of a pull, but I had invested so much time, energy, and emotion into getting this meeting, I couldn't let it go.

"I'm sorry, but I have a very important appointment at that exact time. I can't."

"Oh, that's too bad," she said.

"Thank you for offering—but I have to say no."

She walked away.

I quickly finished my prayers, looked at my watch, and saw that I needed to start heading downtown. The commissioner's office is in Midtown Manhattan on Park Avenue, between 46th and 47th. In the city that never sleeps, it's a busy area anytime, on any day. But the day of my meeting, that area was brutal with traffic because of the Pope's visit.

I walked out of the church, headed down the steps to the sidewalk, and pulled my phone out. I saw that I had missed a call from Major League Baseball. I had turned my phone off before going in to pray. I listened to the voice message. It was the executive I was supposed to meet with.

"Hi, Dan. Sorry to give you such late notice. But with the Pope in town today and traffic so terrible, I'm going to head out a bit early. Let's reschedule for some time next week. Just call my office and set it up with my assistant."

Before I finished walking down the steps, I turned around and ran back into the church to look for the red-haired woman. She was gone. It had taken me two or three minutes, max, to finish praying, get up, walk out, and check my messages. I don't know if she was one of those guardian angels to whom I missed an opportunity to show hospitality, or if she found someone else who accepted the ticket. Whoever she was, she was no longer anywhere to be seen in the church. I had to accept the fact—I had just missed my chance for an audience with the Holy Father.

This story reminds me of a couple of quotations I've heard.

"When someone offers you a seat on a rocket ship, don't ask which seat. Just get on."

I was so focused on what I wanted to come out of this meeting, I never considered that God might have had something even better in mind for me that afternoon. If only I had been willing to sacrifice my plan.

The great Winston Churchill once said, "Optimists are those who see the opportunity in every difficulty. Pessimists see the difficulty in every opportunity."

I've always prided myself on being an optimist. But I had my pessimist pants on that afternoon in St. Jean Baptiste Church.

The next week, I had my meeting. I got to tell the Major League Baseball executive my whole story of coaching and seeing kids get excited and committed to our game. He listened attentively, thanked me for coming in, and I never heard another word from him or anyone in the League offices about it.

I learned a hard lesson in that situation—we may think we know what we want from God. Sometimes we can control events, and try to control people, to make what we want happen; but if we remain open, if we're willing to watch and listen for the God moments, our lives can be much richer and more fulfilling. I've learned to ask God for what I need, and not so much for what I want.

One of my most life-changing pulls from the Holy Spirit came just a couple of years ago. I call it an awakening—my discovery of a newfound faith.

My wife, Heather, had gone to an event at Delbarton called "Come and See." It was hosted by Dr. David Hajduk, a man with tremendous spiritual energy, who oversees the youth ministry at the school. This was the first of three events for that school year. A speaker would give a talk on a particular subject, and then someone else would tell a story from their past to illustrate the topic.

I was working in my home office when she got home from the event. She was so excited about her experience. The topic that night was "Gratitude." As she told me what happened and its impact on her, somehow I knew that I was supposed to give one of those talks. And I knew what I was supposed to talk about.

Forgiveness.

It was time for me to share my story with others. I met with Dr. Hajduk. I told him some of the most intimate moments of my life and how the Lord had dealt with me and my need to forgive my father. I went on to tell him the other times that God had sent his guardian angels to speak to me, to direct me, to lead me where He wanted me to go. I volunteered to speak at the next "Come and See" event. He told me he would pray about it and what the next subject was.

Can you guess?

Forgiveness.

Dr. Hajduk confirmed it, and I spoke briefly, maybe five minutes or so. The response was tremendous. Healing was taking place not only in others but also in me.

Deacon Bill DeVizio, from St. Lawrence Parish in nearby Chester, heard my talk and asked me to come speak at their next "Dinner with the Deacons" event. Rather than a quick five-minute talk, he told me I had half an hour or so to tell my whole story, along with a question and answer session with everyone at the dinner. Once again, the response was overwhelming.

Deacon Bill told me, "Dan, God is using you as his Stradivarius."

I thought he had just called me a dinosaur. But after looking up what that was, I was humbled by the compliment.

Just after I spoke, I was given a brochure for a Cornerstone men's retreat. I was gracious as I accepted the invitation, but in my mind, I was thinking, *Retreats aren't for me.*

I wasn't so sure about going to a weekend retreat with a bunch of men I didn't know. First of all, I can count on one hand how many nights Heather and I have been away from each other. I enjoy my friends' company, but at the end of each night, I want to return home to my family. I argued with myself about going.

Yes, I gave a talk and opened my soul, but I am not that religious guy.

The Cornerstone brochure didn't go into the trashcan—it landed in a bunch of papers on my desk. Somehow it made its way to the top of the pile three months later, just days before the retreat in Morristown.

I looked, I read it, and before I realized what I was doing, I said, *Yes.*

Wow.

The men on this journey, the ones who attended before me and those who will come after, all share a tight bond. These friendships form with God at the center.

We all have friends from childhood, from our communities, from our businesses. Some come and go, some stick around, some last a lifetime. I describe the friendships formed through this retreat as eternal. There is no hidden agenda. Young and old, Black and White, rich and poor, men from all different backgrounds, all with a yearning to be closer to their God, came together to learn, to share, to pray.

Even so, I was uncomfortable at times, especially when it came to prayer—what I prayed for, and who I prayed for, was between God and me.

Until a Bible verse, the words of our Lord, jumped out at me.

For where two or three are gathered together in my name, there am I in the midst of them (Matthew 18:19).

I experienced the presence of Jesus when I was with these godly men. At the end of our prayer sessions, there was an opportunity for people to ask the group to pray for a loved one—someone battling a disease or a very difficult situation. I thought, *If I'm willing to pray with my newfound brothers for people close to them, why shouldn't I allow them to pray with me?*

Finally, I was able to step in comfortably and ask my brothers for their prayers.

These men, these disciples of Jesus Christ, are not perfect. But I draw from their strength, and I have been told that I add to theirs. The following year, I returned as a member of the Cornerstone team.

Standing in front of a crowd I never met and sharing in this intimate and vulnerable way was something I never before had the courage to do. And yet, here I was, having done it several times with ease. I had already moved, after that Saturday morning experience in the car, to a willingness to share one-on-one with friends and strangers alike my faith and God's goodness. Now, it was time for me to stand boldly before groups of people to tell the Good News of Christ as I had experienced Him in my own life. God was calling me to a new place of service.

Along with speaking before groups about my faith, I also felt led to make a public statement in my neighborhood. Every morning before I head downstairs, I look out my bedroom window. I began to have a vision of a cross in the back of our property, up high, blending in with the trees. I could see it—like it had been suspended in the air. I tried to forget it. But I kept thinking, *If I can put a thirty-foot flag pole in the front of my house as a symbol of my patriotism and love of country, of my respect for those who fought and died for the freedom I enjoy, then why can't I share my love for God, for Jesus, with a sixteen-foot cross in my backyard?*

This was one of the few times, if not the only time, I chose not to run my idea by Heather. I headed to The Home Depot with rope in hand.

My plan was to buy the tallest four-by-four they had, which turned out to be sixteen feet, and then use an eight-foot board for the cross piece. After spending several minutes asking one of the workers how deep I would need to bury the bottom of this massive four-by-four for stability, I decided I didn't want to put it in the ground. I would lose too much of the height.

My shed in the backyard is on a concrete slab. I decided to get a four-by-four metal sleeve, which the beam could fit into, and I screwed that down into the concrete behind the seven-foot high shed. This gave me the entire sixteen feet of height and allows everyone to see nine feet of the cross rising in the air.

I managed, using a table saw, to dado out a section of both the vertical and horizontal pieces (thanks for the lesson, Mr. E!). I glued and screwed them together. When I walked the 250 feet or so from my garage to the backyard, carrying that very heavy cross, I thought of what Jesus did on Good Friday. After receiving thirty-nine lashes with a cat-of-nine-tails and having a crown of two-inch thorns crammed on His head, He carried that cross, with Simon of Cyrene's help, to Calvary. He did that for you and me. Thinking of Him, I knew I could make it to the back of our shed with my cross.

Why did I do it? Maybe it's for a kid who comes and gets a baseball lesson in our backyard batting cage. Maybe it's for someone riding down the street, struggling to make sense of things, asking for a sign. Maybe it's for that person who's doubting, questioning. For whomever and for whatever reason, it's there—a giant cross in the middle of the woods, with a light shining on it brightly at night. One neighbor sent Heather an email.

"The cross is shining in my bedroom window."

When Heather told me, at first I thought, *Oh, no, I've upset a neighbor!*

But then she continued.

"It's beautiful!" the neighbor said.

That cross helped me during my recovery from COVID-19. I believe it helped my family while I was in the hospital. I believe it can serve as a symbol, a testimony of Christ being ever present with us, for anyone who sees it.

I'm here. I'm listening.

Jesus whispers those words to me when I look out my window and see it.

We never know the complete ripple effect that our words or actions can have. I still find myself at peace when I see the cross standing straight and tall, even during the strongest windstorm.

In October of 2019, at Delbarton's Homecoming, I ran into Msgr. Geno's brother. He told me that the priest who had married us, who had been so important in the life of Heather's family, was doing great things in Paterson as the Rector of St. John the Baptist. It's the oldest Catholic Church in our state and just a few miles from our home. The next day, Heather and I attended mass at the Cathedral—we haven't missed one since. We were blown away by the love that permeated this building, which is in the middle of one of the toughest neighborhoods in New Jersey.

Across from the front steps of the Cathedral is the Passaic County Jail. If you exit a side door, one of the largest food shelters in the state is directly in front of you. The neighborhood is saturated with crime, poverty, and addiction, but the spirit of the parishioners makes you feel like you're in a slice of Heaven. This primarily Hispanic congregation can't get enough of spreading God's love, crossing the aisles to pass the peace during mass.

Before COVID hit, a young teenaged girl embraced Heather with a sisterly hug that warmed my soul. We love the people in this home away from home, and the Monsignor's gift for spreading the Gospel's message is contagious. We're thrilled to be reunited with our old friend, whose leadership and passion for helping the poor, the lonely, the sick, the disabled, and the addicted inspires us all to love our neighbors as ourselves.

Msgr. Geno refers to this oasis in the heart of Paterson as the "block of mercy."

The history of the building tells the story. In the nineteenth century, volunteers built the Cathedral in just five years in an effort to provide for the growing number of Catholics in the city. In the twentieth century, a need for a gymnasium, a place where children can play safely, was met. I certainly can relate to a kid having a chance to avoid the pitfalls that a tough urban environment presents.

Now, in the twenty-first century, a need has been identified for a new educational and catechetical building to complete this important mission. Soon, Paterson's oasis will provide training and nourishment for the spirit, the mind, and the body—a place where families can play, learn, and worship. Most importantly, they will have a safe haven from a neighborhood that can crush dreams in an instant.

Dear to the heart of our family, especially with Heather's teaching experience, is that a portion of the building will be for special needs children. It will be a facility used to form people in the faith, to recognize that they are loved by God. Once they understand that, like many of us have experienced for ourselves, they will be prepared to share that love with others. Msgr. Geno tells us, "Love opens one to faith. And faith sustains love."

Heather and I have chosen to get actively involved in the campaign to raise funds for this much needed completion of the "block of mercy."[1]

After keeping my faith private for over forty years, I'm now quite bold. I'll shout it from the rooftops for everyone to hear. I've learned from speaking at various parishes and events, and on Catholic radio and television, that there are times when people need to hear about our faith from someone other than their priest. Of course, we need our priests and pastors, our spiritual shepherds, to lead and guide us in the way; but the Holy Spirit is ready and willing to use someone who's married, with kids, with doubts and fears—someone who has fallen short many times—to speak into other people's lives.

Someone with a newfound faith.

Someone like me.

---

1.   If your spirit moves you to help with this very important project, please visit buildingontradition.org. Thank you in advance for your consideration.

CHAPTER FOURTEEN

COVID-19—FAITH, FOCUS, FITNESS, AND HYDROXYCHLOROQUINE

A man only begins to be a man when he ceases to whine and revile and commences to search for the hidden justice which regulates his life. And he adapts his mind to that regulating factor, he ceases to accuse others as the cause of his condition, and builds himself up in strong and noble thoughts; ceases to kick against circumstances, but begins to use them as aids to his more rapid progress, and as a means of the hidden powers and possibilities within himself.

– James Allen, *As a Man Thinketh*

On Friday, March 27, 2020, I didn't feel so great. In fact, I hadn't felt well for three days. Now, I had a terrible headache. I was coughing and feeling achy. Heather insisted that I take my temperature—I was running a fever of 103. I kept thinking:

It's nothing.
I'll get over it.
It's just a bad cold.

Eventually, I had to accept it—there was every indication that I had COVID-19. I had read that if your fever continued for three days, you should get tested. On day six, I drove myself to the local urgent care center. My test came back positive. When I asked what I should do, they told me to stay home, to quarantine myself.

"What about my family?"

"We must assume that they have it as well. They should remain quarantined also."

"What can I take to feel better? The headaches, the achiness, the fever—it's awful!"

"Tylenol."

I had been taking Tylenol since the fever started. It hadn't done squat to alleviate any of my symptoms.

When I told my brother John that I had the coronavirus, he told me about several of his infected friends who had taken hydroxychloroquine. They had improved almost immediately. On Palm Sunday, he tried to get me to make an appointment at the facility on Staten Island where his friends had been treated. That's when I called my friend, Dr. Thorne.

At his urging, I drove myself to the hospital emergency room and was admitted.

Chills, shivering, fatigue, weakness, tightness in my chest, shortness of breath, and excruciating pain every time I moved even slightly—I joined a very long list of people all over the world who were suffering. My symptoms were a combination of all of the above, along with that sledgehammer banging in my head.

The muscle aches were like none I'd ever endured. I've put my body to the test throughout my life—in the gym, on my bike, on the base paths. Now, for the first time in my life, my muscles wouldn't, or couldn't, respond to my commands. They were heavy—not cramp-like, but sore to the touch, as if I had been tackled over and over by a 300-pound lineman or checked repeatedly against the boards in the hockey rink.

Those first hours in the hospital, I was fading. I could feel my temperature rising, and my breathing was going from bad to worse. I felt like I was in competition with my roommate, fighting for the attention of the valiant workers who would come in with their plastic shields, gloves, and masks. Where am I? How did I get here? Delirium from the fever set in.

Somehow, I managed to get through that first night, but now I was obsessed with getting out—like immediately. I had gotten, *maybe,* a total of one hour of sleep, in about four fifteen-minute segments. The first thing the next morning, I asked the doctor to release me.

"You had a one hundred and four-degree fever last night. We can't send you home. Let's give it some time."

I went over my escape route in my now 103-degree mind. Wisdom ruled, however, and I decided to listen to Dr. Thorne's advice and stick with the plan.

"Sir, you have to turn over. You can't stay on your back all day and all night; this is not helpful to your breathing."

I heard the nurse say this to my roommate through the thin curtain that separated us. He was struggling. They had asked him to use his breathing gadget, but in the twelve hours or so that we shared the room, I heard him use it just once. He never got out of his bed. For his bathroom needs, they came to him. The only time he perked up was when he received a FaceTime call from his son, his daughter-in law, who spoke to him in Spanish (a concerned voice sounds the same in any language), and his grandchildren. I believe they were showing him cards that they made for him.

"Pop, you don't sound so good," his son said.

I could tell the son was frustrated, trying to get information from the busy staff. I wished I could tell him what I knew—I had insider information. His father was going downhill fast. Only moments after they hung up, he was wheeled out of the room. Our eyes met for the first time—a glance, a nod—and then I said a prayer for this poor guy who did not have the physical strength to fight.

I don't know if he was unwilling or unable—but I determined to learn from him. I needed to move around the room. I needed to use that little torturous incentive spirometer—the breathing apparatus. And I needed to lie on my stomach. He had done none of the above, and he was taken to the ICU—to the dreadful ventilator. We learned later that it might as well have been a death sentence.

I couldn't get the room-temperature water down, but I drank pitchers of ice water all day long. I needed to stay hydrated. I also needed fuel, and not just the mental and spiritual fuel that was about to come my way from so many different directions. I needed to get nourishment to my depleted muscles, whatever was left of them.

When I couldn't stomach the standard hospital food they brought me, Anne, one of the health practitioners, came in to take my order for a custom-made sandwich.

"Turkey, lettuce, and tomato, please," I said.

"What kind of bread would you like?" she asked.

Manna from one of God's guardian angels came down to give me the physical fuel I needed.

Monday night, April 6th, my fever broke and did not return. What Tylenol couldn't touch over a twelve-day span, hydroxychloroquine had vanquished in twenty-four hours.

Would I have gotten better with traditional care? The only way to know would be to go back in time and not take it. But I would not go back, unless I had a do-over that enabled me to take it even sooner.

Still, with the fever gone, I was far from being back to myself. Since contracting COVID, I had lost twenty-five pounds. I wasn't carrying any excess weight to start—my body was shedding necessary muscle. This made the simple tasks I needed to perform beyond challenging. They asked me to breathe into the spirometer ten times an hour—I did it at least twenty. Every hour, on the hour, I got myself out of bed. Just doing that felt like the hardest workout I had ever done.

I have spent twenty-plus years staying fit as a professional athlete and a trainer. I know about the power of having a strong body—I've helped sculpt them for my clients, and I had sculpted my own. And from my years as a player and as a life coach, I knew quite a bit about focus.

I had the playbook. I knew what didn't work from my long list of mistakes, and I knew how to apply those things that did. I needed to understand the goals. What's the *why* behind them? Once I understand the why, then I can:

Set the goal.
Write it down.
Visualize meeting it.
Take the necessary action.

That's what Michael Jordan did before he took the shot, what Derek Jeter did before he got the hit. It's what I had done before every pitch was thrown while I was on the field. I would visualize the ball being hit to my right or left and then diving to catch it. Maybe this is why I made more diving catches than my teammates or opponents.

This proved to be the toughest challenge on that first day in the hospital. COVID was doing everything in its power to keep me on my back. I needed to share my goals, to keep myself accountable. I shared them with everyone who came in the room.

"I am going home today."

I said it to the cleaning crew, to the doctors who probably laughed at my optimism. I said it every day until it worked.

Before I had a chance to write down my goals, a care package came from Heather. Next to the mound of protein bars, my breathing spirometer, a pitcher of ice water, my phone, and a couple of bottles of Poland Spring that I used as one-pound dumbbells, went the best thing she could have sent me—a picture of our family. Coach Heather knows me well. That picture was more powerful than writing down my desire to get home to them. It stayed in plain view on my table along with the rest of my arsenal. She and both boys also made me homemade get-well cards. I set my heart and mind to fulfill their message.

My physical strength had been ravaged. It would require much more than mere physical fitness for me to beat this insidious enemy. Yes, I would need to apply what I had learned about fitness. To that, I had to add what I had learned about focus. Still not enough. To those I needed to add not only my own faith, but the faith of others to stand with me in prayer.

I learned that Msgr. Geno led five thousand people, who tuned in by satellite to the Cathedral's online service, in prayers for me. I get teary just thinking about that! I turned the channel on the television from the dreadful news spewing out and stopped when I heard the words Jesus taught us to pray. Mother Angelica led us in the Lord's Prayer, in the Hail Mary, in the Holy Rosary. God used her as one of my angels in that hospital room.

I prayed along with her for thirty minutes or so, and those prayers gave me the spiritual strength and comfort I needed to attack that day of exercises—to face Corona head-on. As I lasered in on my mission, an influx of text messages and emails started coming in.

From my friend, Rob DeBrino:

Praying for you, my brother! Sent out prayer chain across the country, told my mom, we've got a lot of people praying for you and your family.

He forwarded me a text from his friend who was a cardiologist.

Make sure you turn him into prone position on his stomach; it helps oxygenation and healing of lungs.

I knew this, but I didn't want to. It hurt too much. COVID and the little red guy on my left shoulder put me in too comfortable a position, on my back and relatively pain-free. To roll over meant inflicting hellish pain on myself.

I've been flipping, bro, but it's been a battle, I said.

I got messages every single day from Chad, my workout partner with the Twins:

Kick that Mother*&^&%&'s ass!

Subtlety was never Chad's strong suit.

You will beat this! You're the toughest SOB I ever played with!

See what I mean? But his words of encouragement spurred me on.

Dr. Thorne checked in to see how I was doing.

Hurts when I breathe in deep, I said.

He texted right back.

I know it hurts to breathe deeply. Do it anyway. If you have the strength, stand at your bedside a few times a day, take deep breaths even though it hurts and even stretch your arms above your head.

You've got this.

The virus wants you to lie down and let it take over your body; don't let it!

Thinking about you and sending healing vibrations your way.

The physical challenge was tough, but three things helped me. I forced myself to get up and move around the room, used water bottles as dumbbells, and I did chair squats. Second, I used the incentive spirometer to help expand my lungs. Lastly, I stayed in the prone position, on my stomach for as long as I could tolerate it, and then some. That was difficult in a hospital bed.

I zoned in. In baseball, it's called the "flow experience"— those times when the ball looks like a beach ball. I've had this moment reoccur throughout most of my baseball career. I also had it when I met and married Heather. It's a moment of unstoppable confidence. It's a feeling I wish everyone could have. Even though the physical tasks seemed impossible, there was no way I would not accomplish them. I was so clear on the mission, like a soldier taking orders from his commander.

Every thirty minutes I did a circuit of weight training—first just using my body weight, and then I graduated a few hours later to the one pounders (water bottles) and stuck with them for a few days. I did shoulder presses and bicep curls while I was in the bed. I now had the room to myself, since my roommate left for the ICU.

God had given me all the training, all the tools at my disposal that I would need to draw on. All of those days that one season with Coach Mel, those days of training my body with the goal of becoming a big leaguer. All the lessons I had learned from science, from literature, from motivational speakers, from my coaches, and from the Bible. Humanism, science, and faith intertwined to empower my spirit, my mind, and my body.

Faith.
Focus.
Fitness.

They acted together in perfect harmony, like a symphony or orchestra, like the beauty of synchronized swimming, like a perfectly executed ballet.

I got this.

I pulled that little charm up from my chain, the Christ head that did a head stand when I faced my first battle with near death in the head-on collision. I felt the sharp edge of Jesus's hair that had stuck in me. Now, I stuck to him in the same way.

Our minds will play tricks on us. Every day in that hospital, at some point, I wanted to just lie on my back and stop with that little thing they call breathing. It was tougher than hitting any ninety-mile-per-hour fastball, tougher than any grueling workout I had given myself or my clients. As soon as the thought of a ventilator, an extended stay in the hospital, and even death crept in, I tackled it with the right visualization, with concentration techniques, with unfazed focus.

I remembered a breathing technique I had learned that helped me settle down.

This was by far the most difficult. COVID had already entered my lungs—pneumonia had set in. I would take a breath, or as much as I could, and hold it. Then I would exhale for three to four times longer. This put me in a relaxed state, a place where I could think more clearly about the tasks before me.

Eat. Hydrate. Move.

My cardio workout was a trip to the window. I thought about changing my position in the room to be next to it, but I felt better being closer to the bathroom and, more importantly, to the exit. That window, however, was significant to my recovery. I pulled the curtain open. Now I had my own workout area with the sun shining through. It's amazing how we take the sun's light for granted. I couldn't hear the sounds of God's creatures on the other side of the window, but I could see them.

Blue jays, cardinals, doves, sparrows—I marveled at their freedom, at their good health. I sat in a chair by the window during my rest periods (the ten-foot walk to get there felt like my usual ten-mile bike ride). While my body was recouping and regaining strength, my spirit and soul were reflecting.

I watched the hospital heroes come and go outside—masks on, masks off—as these doctors, nurses, and health care workers arrived and departed from the hospital parking lot. Arriving to see people like me plagued with a horrific condition. Departing to see their families, after what was never *just another day at the office.*

I thought about having Heather drive with the boys to a spot in the parking lot, or just by the curb. I watched couples walking hand in hand, longing to be back with the love of my life. I watched boys on their bikes, probably heading home to have dinner with their families. I thought of our precious family dinners. I was determined to be back at that table.

"Always give one hundred percent."

There was Coach Harry in my ear—time to do more chair squats. How many times have I had my clients do squats like these? At first, I couldn't do one without using my upper body. Still, I made sure I did all ten, allowing my other muscles to help as much as needed. They all chipped in, helping—my legs were just too weak to do it on their own.

There's a spiritual lesson for us! We were not created to get along on our own. We need one another. As the poet and Anglican priest John Donne wrote, "No man is an island." Msgr. Geno often says, "As Catholics, we never journey alone." Our connections, our support, our encouragement for one another is life-giving.

Each exercise routine, I went a little bit further. I kept pushing the goal line. For three nights, I had the room to myself. I worked up to jogging in place for ten minutes without oxygen. After each exercise, I allowed time for a break. There were many times that I thought:

Will I ever get my strength back?

Then I would hear Msgr. Geno.

"Never feel sorry for yourself."

Back to another set. As soon as a negative thought came in, I had an army of God's soldiers, my angels, both living and dead, storming heaven's gates for me and whispering in my ear.

Kick this thing's ass!

The caring hospital staff constantly checked my O2 levels, both with and without the oxygen. I would take it off for periods at a time, but those first days I needed it to breathe comfortably. I knew that without it, my numbers dropped. They wouldn't let me leave until I was able to exercise in the room at a decent level. They wanted to see me walk circles in the room, to jog in place.

I trained myself, the way I did others for well over thirty thousand hours in my life.

Five more.

I figured I said those two words to my clients at least six hundred thousand times. Now I needed to make sure I did those extra reps.

I thought back to all those training sessions when I pushed my clients to go just a little bit further, those years of training myself as a professional athlete, and even before then.

Dreams become goals when you write them down and have a plan.

And only when you put that plan into action do they become a reality.

I frequently felt like an old car running on fumes. Minute by minute, however, I began to see results—nothing that would allow me to run a marathon mind you, but I began to get more air into my lungs. My first walk had been to the bathroom—about a three-foot walk, which took me thirteen steps (okay, they were more like shuffles) to complete. By Wednesday, I felt good enough to get rid of fourteen days' worth of scruff on my face, give myself a washcloth once over, clip my nails, and clean myself up.

Early Thursday morning, they came in to give me my test. I crushed it!

"Mister Venezia, your O2 levels are good. We can send you home today, and we don't need to send you home with oxygen."

Rather than ICU and a ventilator, I was going home. I knew that my fitness training, my focus work as a life coach, my faith as a disciple of Jesus Christ all worked together to get me to that moment.

But there was a fourth element to my salvation from COVID-19:

Hydroxychloroquine.

Some people told me that I shouldn't talk about it—it's too controversial. But why should it be? During this pandemic, too many people have had their stories of healing, of being saved from death by taking this eighty-six year old malaria drug. I'm not a doctor or a scientific research professional. And I'm not a politician with a party platform to polemicize.

I'm just a guy. A former professional baseball player, a fitness trainer and life coach, a bold proclaimer of the Good News of Jesus Christ, and a husband and father who after four days got to go home to his wife and two teenaged boys. Faith, focus, fitness, and hydroxychloroquine saved me from COVID-19.

On Thursday morning, they wheeled in my second roommate. I was packed up, however, waiting on my discharge papers, and ready to give him his own private room. Before I left, I said, "Make sure you turn on your stomach, and use that spirometer, even if it hurts."

I was back to being Coach Dan.

He was too sick to respond.

I hope he wasn't too sick to listen.

Anne, the guardian angel who made me my sandwiches, wheeled me down the hallway and out of the hospital. I had been fever-free for three straight days, and my headaches were gone. Even though I was still a bit achy with a slight cough, I was on my way back to good health. I felt confident yet humbled by the compassion of dozens of doctors, nurses, cleaning crew, and other members of the hospital staff. I recognized them through their protective shields as they lined the hallway, clapping for me! I should have been the one clapping for them.

A verse came into my head, which I kept thinking about:

Today you will be with me in paradise.

Finally, I looked it up—it's in Luke's Gospel, chapter twenty-three, verse forty-three. Luke 23:43.

I see that as a promise to everyone—it's never too late to turn to Christ. One thief chose to mock Jesus. He wouldn't, or couldn't because of the hardness of his heart, recognize God in the flesh. But for that other thief, with his dying breath, he said to Jesus:

Remember me when you come into your kingdom.

God in the flesh, in his dying mercy from that cross, didn't require the thief to clean up his act or do anything other than ask. And God gave him an answer for all of eternity.

I asked, I got my answer, and I met my goal—I was able to get out of that hospital bed and go home to my family. By the way—my hospital room number was 2343!

CHAPTER FIFTEEN

EASTER SUNDAY— RESURRECTION

As I was leaving the hospital, I couldn't wait to get to my car in the parking lot and drive home.

But then I stopped. Just outside the open doors—my exit to freedom and pathway to my family—were petunias in a flower bed. Magenta, violet, purple—a myriad of spring colors. Just seeing them made me feel such joy. Instead of sprinting to my car, I stopped to "smell the roses." Okay—the petunias.

How often had I blown past such a simple reminder of God's creative love of beauty, of order, of life itself? I felt like I was one with His landscape. I wasn't out of the woods by any means, but I was present. Content with my lot—eager to share my story with the world.

I'm not sure how long I stayed there without moving. From where I stood, I tried to smell those flowers, as if I needed to maintain a six-foot distance from them, the space we've adopted since COVID stopped our world. As time stood still, in that moment I experienced a pain-free awakening. The scent of the flowers permeated a wonderful breeze that came down the corridor, and in one clean sweep the aroma from this colorful arrangement washed over me.

It was as if God himself had given a subtle, yet powerful, exhale. I took it in, with a breath that didn't hurt. I looked up and smiled. I had so much to be thankful for. Now, truly released, I was free to walk to my car.

I arrived home that Holy Thursday at 3:15 p.m. Even though I was three days without fever, the medical team wanted me to continue to quarantine. It was so hard to not hug my wife and my sons when I walked in the door! But I exercised the necessary discipline and returned to my bedroom—an oasis compared to that hospital room. I had to be satisfied with visits from my gang of three standing in the doorway. They came often with food and good wishes. No longer did I only have them with me in a picture on the bedside table—they were there, in flesh and blood, their smiles and love infusing me with more strength to recover.

Heather told me how family, friends, and acquaintances had all come together to help her and the boys while I was absent. Gift cards for food, meals dropped off, constant prayers. They came from clients, from neighbors, from old teammates, friends, and extended family, who all reached out with love and care.

I knew I couldn't let being home bring complacency. I had to maintain and intensify my workout routine to get my strength back. I upgraded to Heather's three-pound dumbbells on Good Friday. I also exercised my spirit that day by watching Mel Gibson's *The Passion of the Christ*.

What a reminder! My battle? A walk in the park compared to what our Lord endured on the cross for us. Each day I'm reminded to look out my bedroom window, to the cross in our backyard, and thank Him for paying the debt I could never repay. The debt *we* could never repay—our sin, our shame, our regrets and past mistakes, our unforgiveness, our hurt and anger—by His Good Friday act of love and sacrifice, He marked it all for every one of us—

Paid in full.

Easter Sunday morning, I woke up to the sound of an angelic choir outside my window. A chorus of birds, singing as beautifully as any performance of Handel's *Messiah*, greeted the dawn of Resurrection Day. The sun beamed through my curtains, and I felt its warmth. For the first time in three weeks, since my first symptom, I truly felt better.

I got up, showered, and even though I would be attending Easter Mass online from my bedroom quarantine, I decided to dress in my Sunday clothes. Heather was shocked when she saw them hanging off me like they belonged to someone else. COVID had stolen a good percentage of my body weight. I knew it would take time to regain it. But with the lockdown and being quarantined, I now had plenty of time on my hands.

The definition in my arms was gone. My core muscles had disappeared. But I knew they would return. By Saturday, I was using Heather's five-pound dumbbells. Easter Sunday after-noon, I moved up to the eight-pounders. Remember:

Keep at it, stay consistent.

I applied the same discipline to my morning prayers.

I used to keep my alarm clock under my bed. I did that for two reasons—one, so I wouldn't hit the snooze button, but most importantly, so I would have to get down on my knees to turn it off.

After surviving COVID-19, I no longer have to put my alarm clock under my bed. I don't need the reminder to get on my knees, to be thankful for the gift of each day. I start with a deep breath, a big one—I appreciate each one I take, so very much.

Think about it—do you ever stop to be thankful for the gift of being able to breathe? Science tells us that breathing is an involuntary response—our bodies just do it without our having to think about it. But let me tell you—when it gets hard, when we feel like we can't breathe, boy, do we think about it!

Throughout the course of my day now, I breathe in deeply, recalling those struggling COVID moments, say a prayer of thanks, and invite God's peace to flow into me.

The Tuesday after Easter, Heather and I hugged. As powerful as that first hug was on the pier during our first date, and the thousands that we've given one another over the years, this one was different. I got another swing of the bat. A batter pops up in foul territory, thinks he's out, and then somehow the ball evades the glove of the fielder. That batter gets another swing. I was still alive at the plate. And it felt so good!

In India, there is a tale of a man who would pray in the Ganges River. One day he noticed a venomous scorpion trying to survive, grasping for a twig. The man scooped it up and was stung immediately. The next day, the same creature again was struggling in the river to save itself. The man came to its rescue, and once again was stung. The scorpion then said, "Why are you saving me? Don't you know by now that I will sting you every time, because that is what I do?"

The man again placed it on safe ground and replied, "Because this is what I do."

It's a perfect illustration of our relationship with God. We mess up, we fall, we sin, we sting; but every time, if we will allow Him, He will pick us up, embrace us, and place us on safe ground.

Putting order in our lives, especially in times of stress and turmoil, is not always easy. Through all that I have experienced, I have learned that in those times, having that order, and our priorities in line, is even more important than we can imagine.

As I look back over my life, I had order, but not always in its proper sequence. From a chronological perspective, my life's order has been Fitness, Focus, and Faith. Body, Mind, and Spirit. Each important. Each one necessary and significant in my surviving COVID.

But from my perspective today, looking back on my experience, I see that my order was skewed. I now know this, and, more than anything else, I can share with you.

You need to get this order right:

Spirit. Mind. Body.
Faith. Focus. Fitness.

Put God first in everything you do!

These bodies we live in are temporary. Sure, I've survived COVID. And God willing, I have many decades left to walk around in my body. But my spirit? That is what will carry me into eternity!

I hope and pray that my story will be a source of encouragement and inspiration to you. Perhaps you need to work on your fitness, to add some discipline in that area of your life. In order to maintain your fitness, applying the focus techniques I learned and discussed in Chapter Twelve will surely help.

But if you only get one thing from reading my book, I pray it will be a motivation to embrace and build up your faith. We can never have too much!

Here's one more God moment.

While writing this book, every morning I would jot down ideas for future chapters in a Google document on my phone. One particular morning, I thought of a Christmas card we sent out fourteen years ago. It read:

Blessed are those who see Christmas through the eyes of a child.

The phrase kept going over and over in my mind. I played with the words a bit, wondering if I should paraphrase it in some way. Here's what I wrote:

Maybe I should say, "Blessed are those who see the 'world' through the eyes of a child"

or

"Blessed are those who see 'God' through the eyes of a child."

And then this appeared:

✝

That very symbol of a cross, right at the end of my notes.

Sure, sometimes letters or symbols get punched in by accident. But I had no idea where that cross came from!

I even typed everything over again to see if it would appear. Nothing. And I haven't been able to find it as part of the emojis or symbols on my phone.

You may think it's nothing. And that's fine.

But I received it as one more confirmation from God of His presence with me, His leading and guiding me to tell my story, and to give me hope that He would use me to bring healing and wholeness to anyone who reads this book.

If you look at the cover, in the word FAI✝H, you'll notice the cross replaces the letter T. The cross reminds me to be on the lookout, and not to miss, another God moment.

The Christ-head pendant after the head-on collision.
The traffic on the Garden State Parkway causing me to get off sixteen miles early.

The man on Park Avenue telling me I belonged in baseball.

The woman with the red hair offering me a ticket to see the Pope.

The inspiration to ask for hydroxychloroquine when I got to the hospital.

These are only a handful of mine. What are yours? Are there any that you might have missed? Don't miss another one—life is too precious. Ask Him to help you:

Train your spirit for Faith.
Train your mind for Focus.
Train your body for Fitness.

And I pray you never need hydroxychloroquine.

ACKNOWLEDGMENTS

To the Holy Trinity—Father, Son, and Holy Spirit,
I see my Father's presence in the likeness and beauty of all His children;

I hear the whisper of Jesus in my thoughts and in my prayers; I feel the power of the Holy Spirit with every breath I take.

To Heather—You've stuck with me and by me through all of life's ups and downs. In twenty-plus years, there hasn't been a day I didn't want to come home. I am so very much in love with you. You are an amazing wife, mother, and friend. I look forward to the memories we will continue to make and share with one another. You are my everything!

To Ryan and Skyler—You both have brought me pure JOY. Stay intellectually curious, be good stewards of the gifts you've been given, and always keep your eyes on the prize. I am so glad God picked me to be your dad!

To Mom—You may have been given a bad break with some tough years early on, but it never kept you from holding our family together. You were my first role model for how to combine faith, a strong work ethic, and mental toughness, not allowing the hard knocks of life to keep me down. You taught me how to love, not by words but by actions. You are my rock.

To my biological father—I pray for you every day. I hope that your heart is softened and you hand it over to Jesus. He is waiting for you, and He is forgiving.

To my siblings—John, for stepping in and helping our family the way you did when I was so young. It is a tribute to your strong character. I am grateful that our relationship has grown even closer through the years. Janet, you have always been one of my biggest supporters, and you have been there for me not only as a sister but as a friend. Thanks for always believing in me. James, we are closest in age and share so many childhood memories. Your heart is huge, and your intentions are always good. I hope you know I'll always be there for you, no matter what! I'm so grateful for our closeness as a family and the love we share.

To Aunt Jeannie and my late Uncle George—We prayed together during the summer of 1983. Thanks to you both, those prayers continue to have an impact on my spiritual life.

To my late father-in-law, Paul Englehardt—Our twenty years together were too short. I will carry with me the lessons I learned from you the rest of my life. They definitely don't make 'em like you anymore.

To Msgr. Geno—My friend, my priest, my brother. You are a Father in so many ways to all who know you, especially to the parishioners at the Cathedral of St. John the Baptist. Thanks for being a whisper in my ear. You are a bright light, a beacon of hope, a living saint!

To Joe—We've been friends a long time. We met in the schoolyard thirty-five years ago when I picked you last in a choose-up game of punch ball. I never made that mistake again. Love you, brother!

To all my friends and extended family members—Thank you for being there for Heather, the boys, and me, especially while I was battling this virus. I am forever grateful for your acts of kindness, the consistent food deliveries, along with your genuine concern, well wishes, and, most importantly, your prayers.

To all of my clients (you know who you are)—Thank you for your loyalty, your wisdom, and for sharpening my reasoning. Most importantly, thank you for your belief in me. I hope I live up to my end by helping you all in spirit, mind, and body.

To my late scout, Herb Stein, and the Minnesota Twins—Thank you for giving me a shot at my childhood dream. Thanks for the opportunity, but I also thank you for cutting me when you did. It was all part of a plan greater than ours.

To every kid I've ever coached—Don't forget the simple motto, "Be Fair. Play Hard." Remember there are more ways to win than what the scoreboard reads at the end of the game.

To the parents of every player I've ever coached—Thank you for entrusting me with your most prized possessions. I am quite confident I returned your little sluggers with more fitness and focus than when they were dropped off.

To Tim and Amy Berkowitz—I admire your family values, your strong principles, and I am humbled and inspired by your warm and gentle souls. The saying goes, "You become like those you hang around." I should be so lucky!

To my Cornerstone Brothers—We share a bond, which is more than just a lifetime friendship. Our chance meeting was not chance at all. Meeting with no hidden agenda—just a bunch of men looking to be better fathers, husbands, and neighbors—you end up with a foundation with Christ at its center. This is a tough one to crack; therefore, you are my eternal friends.

To Ben Pagano—Your encouragement to make every day a masterpiece is a true blessing. Thank you for reminding me to stay in the moment and in the light while keeping my motives pure. You, my friend, are a breath of fresh air!

To all my Guardian Angels, too many to count—Keep intervening, keep nudging; I do feel your presence.

To Dr. Charles Thorne—You may not have known it at the time, but your sound medical advice helped me defeat this invisible disease. I am forever grateful for your great coaching!

To all health care workers who work around the clock to care for patients, especially those with COVID-19—Your compassion and selfless acts of courage on a daily basis are an inspiration to the world. When most were running away from people with my condition, you were there in the trenches with me. A heartfelt thanks to the staff at Valley Hospital, especially Anne, for your kind and gentle ways.

To the team at Kevin Anderson and Associates—Kevin, I knew from our first conversation that your firm was the right one to get this project started. *The eyes are the windows to the soul.* I knew by looking in yours (even from your website pic since I was still under quarantine) that you were genuine and honest. You've delivered on both counts, along with everything promised. You found the right publisher and delivered on every timeline. A special thanks to our senior editor at KAA, Amanda Ayers Barnett—Your input was spot on. Jacob King—Thank you for managing this project. Finally, to my collaborator, Frederick Richardson—Freddy, you understood what this story was about from the very beginning. There is no doubt that God put us together. Our countless phone calls flowed like we were old friends. You listened, not only with your ears, but with your heart and your mind. Your patience, guidance, and expertise put me at ease. You made sure my thoughts and feelings came through, and that our Lord was front and center every step of the way. Freddy, I am blessed to call you my brother in Christ! And to your wife, Dale—thank you for sharing your husband with me for ten weeks.

A special thanks to Stephen Bienko, Lauren Kelly, and the entire team at 42 Growth Strategies for helping me grow my social media presence.

To Post Hill Press—Thank you for your immediate response to our proposal. Your belief in this manuscript before it was completed and in my ability to be an effective advocate and spokesperson motivated me even more. To Debby Englander—I knew from our first conversation that Post Hill was the right publisher to take on this important project. Debby, you believed in the background of my story, the Catholic perspective, and you were eager to get started right away. You also believed that writing as a Catholic Christian layperson, I would find an audience both in this country and beyond our borders. To the entire editorial and production team, especially Heather King, my managing editor and point person, who helped guide me through the publication process. Thank you all so much!

Lastly, thank you to everyone who prayed for me. I am living proof that your prayers worked!

I've heard deep callings at times in my life. Writing this book was one of them. I hope I've lived up to God's plan with these pages—I have no doubt that the Holy Spirit was the breath behind every word.

ABOUT THE AUTHOR

The youngest of four children raised by a single mom in Brooklyn, Dan Venezia's proficiency at baseball led him to be drafted by the Minnesota Twins after college. Once his dream of making it to the big leagues ended, Dan applied his focused self-discipline to his fitness training and coaching business on Manhattan's Upper East Side. He directs camps and clinics, and gives private lessons throughout the tri-state region, where he also serves as a life coach. Dan's faith in Christ has been strengthened by unique and powerful interventions that God has made in his work, his family life, and his interactions with those less fortunate. A popular and sought-after inspirational speaker, he has had the opportunity to share his story in his parish, his community, and on local, regional, national, and international radio and television programs—from ESPN to Canada's number one talk radio show. Dan's children's book—*Coach Dan on Sportsmanship*—has sold over one thousand copies and encourages young people to experience the joy of sports without the pressure to win at all costs. Not only is Dan a survivor of COVID-19, he is a survivor who took hydroxychloroquine, the controversial drug that saved his life. Dan has a unique story to tell as a former professional baseball player, a successful fitness trainer and coach, a loving husband and father, and a passionate follower of Christ committed to share with others the power of faith, focus, and fitness.

Follow Dan on Instagram @danvenezia23 or visit his website at danvenezia.com.